The Simple Ninja Dual Zone Air Fryer Cookbook UK

2023

1500 Days Fast and Super-Delicious Air Fryer Recipes with Tips & Tricks to Fry, Grill, Roast, Bake & Dehydrate at Ease

Jaiden Kuvalis

Copyright© 2023 By Jaiden Kuvalis

All rights reserved worldwide.
No part of this book may be reproduced or transmitted in any form or by any means, electronic or mechanical, including photo- copying, recording or by any information storage and retrieval system, without written permission from the publisher, except for the inclusion of brief quotations in a review.

Warning-Disclaimer

The purpose of this book is to educate and entertain. The author or publisher does not guarantee that anyone following the techniques, suggestions, tips, ideas, or strategies will become successful. The author and publisher shall have neither liability or responsibility to anyone with respect to any loss or damage caused, or alleged to be caused, directly or indirectly by the information contained in this book.

Table of Contents

INTRODUCTION 1

Chapter 1 Breakfasts 2

Egg Tarts and Mushroom-and-Tomato Stuffed Hash Browns 3
Broccoli-Mushroom Frittata and Sausage Stuffed Peppers 3
Canadian Bacon Muffin Sandwiches and Egg-and-Bacon Muffins 4
Savory Sweet Potato Hash and Spinach-and-Mushroom Mini Quiche 4
Breakfast Sausage and Cauliflower and Nutty Granola 4
Egg in a Hole and Chimichanga Breakfast Burrito 5
Oat-and-Chia Porridge and Pizza Eggs 5
Lemon-Blueberry Muffins and Wholemeal Banana-Walnut Bread 5
Banana-Nut Muffins 6
Jalapeño-and-Bacon Breakfast Pizza and Denver Omelette 6
Breakfast Meatballs and Cauliflower Avocado Toast..... 6
Oat Bran Muffins and Pork Sausage Eggs with Mustard Sauce 7
Honey-Apricot Granola with Greek Yoghurt and Egg White Cups 7
Cinnamon-Raisin Bagels and Scotch Eggs 8
Golden Avocado Tempura and Turkey Breakfast Sausage Patties 8

Chapter 2 Family Favorites 9

Steak and Vegetable Kebabs and Filo Vegetable Triangles 10
Coconut Chicken Tenders and Pork Burgers with Red Cabbage Salad 10
Chinese-Inspired Spareribs and Fried Green Tomatoes... 11
Avocado-and-Egg Burrito and Veggie Tuna Melts   11
Fish-and-Vegetable Tacos and Meatball Subs 11

Chapter 3 Fast and Easy Everyday Favourites 12

Beef Bratwursts and Simple-and-Easy Croutons 13
Cheesy Chilli Toast and Baked Cheese Sandwich 13
Spinach-and-Carrot Balls and Crunchy Fried Okra 13
Buttery Sweet Potatoes and Bacon Pinwheels 14
Herb-Roasted Veggies and Cheesy Jalapeño Cornbread.. 14
Peppery Brown Rice Fritters and Cheesy Potato Patties 14
Rosemary and Orange Roasted Chickpeas 15
Air Fried Shishito Peppers and Easy Devils on Horseback... 15

Chapter 4 Poultry — 16

- Chicken Manchurian and Chicken Paillard 17
- Chicken Schnitzel and Bacon-Wrapped Stuffed Chicken Breasts 17
- Peachy Chicken Chunks with Cherries and Thai Tacos with Peanut Sauce 18
- Chicken, Courgette, and Spinach Salad and South Indian Pepper Chicken 18
- Chicken and Vegetable Fajitas 19
- Coriander Lime Chicken Thighs and Celery Chicken 19
- Potato-Crusted Chicken and Simply Terrific Turkey Meatballs 19
- Piri-Piri Chicken Thighs 20
- Crunchy Chicken Tenders and Lemon-Basil Turkey Breasts 20
- Herb-Buttermilk Chicken Breast and Nice Goulash 20
- Herbed Roast Chicken Breast 21
- Personal Cauliflower Pizzas 21
- Chicken Thighs with Coriander and Bell Pepper Stuffed Chicken Roll-Ups 21
- Stuffed Turkey Roulade 22
- Spice-Rubbed Turkey Breast and Sweet Chili Spiced Chicken 22
- African Piri-Piri Chicken Drumsticks 22
- Chicken Breasts with Asparagus, Beans, and Rocket 23
- Korean Honey Wings 23
- Hoisin Turkey Burgers and Chicken with Pineapple and Peach 23

Chapter 5 Beef, Pork, and Lamb — 24

- Spaghetti Zoodles and Meatballs 25
- Panko Pork Chops 25
- Broccoli and Pork Teriyaki 25
- Kheema Burgers 26
- Mushroom in Bacon-Wrapped Filets Mignons 26
- Greek Lamb Pitta Pockets 26
- Tomato and Bacon Zoodles 26
- Chinese-Style Baby Back Ribs 27
- Sausage and Peppers 27
- Zesty London Broil 27
- Herbed Beef 27
- Lemony Pork Loin Chop Schnitzel 27
- Blue Cheese Steak Salad 28
- Cinnamon-Beef Kofta 28
- Spicy Tomato Beef Meatballs 28
- Vietnamese Grilled Pork 28
- Pork and Tricolor Vegetables Kebabs 29
- Greek-Style Meatloaf 29
- Pork Bulgogi 29
- Air Fried Beef Satay with Peanut Dipping Sauce 29
- Sweet and Spicy Country-Style Ribs 30
- Bacon, Cheese and Pear Stuffed Pork 30
- Italian Pork Loin 30
- Mozzarella Stuffed Beef and Pork Meatballs 30
- Marinated Steak Tips with Mushrooms 31
- Mustard Herb Pork Tenderloin 31
- Garlic-Marinated Bavette Steak 31
- Pork Medallions with Endive Salad 31
- Bean and Beef Meatball Taco Pizza 32
- Simple Beef Mince with Courgette 32

Chapter 6 Fish and Seafood — 33

- Garlic Lemon Scallops 34
- Simple Buttery Cod 34
- Tuna-Stuffed Quinoa Patties 34
- Salmon with Provolone Cheese and Prawn Bake 34
- Salmon Fritters with Courgette and Blackened Fish 35
- Mouthwatering Cod over Creamy Leek Noodles 35
- Cucumber and Salmon Salad and Roasted Halibut Steaks with Parsley 35
- Popcorn Prawns 36
- Ahi Tuna Steaks and Foil-Packet Lobster Tail 36
- Cheesy Tuna Patties and Sea Bass with Potato Scales 36
- Classic Fish Sticks with Tartar Sauce 37
- Oyster Po'Boy and Crunchy Fish Sticks 37
- Pecan-Crusted Catfish and Crab Legs 37
- Tandoori-Spiced Salmon-and-Potatoes and Apple Cider Mussels 38
- Salmon Croquettes and Golden Beer-Battered Cod 38
- Country Prawns and Salmon Spring Rolls 38
- Lemony Prawns-and-Courgette and Sea Bass with Avocado Cream 39
- Cod with Jalapeño and Coconut Prawns with Spicy Dipping Sauce 39

Chapter 7 Snacks and Appetizers — 40

Cheese Drops and Polenta Fries with Chilli-Lime Mayo 41
Cheesy Steak Fries and Baked Spanakopita Dip 41
Italian Rice Balls 42
Authentic Scotch Eggs 42
Taco-Spiced Chickpeas and Greek Potato Skins with Olives-and-Feta 42
Jalapeño Poppers and Greens Chips with Curried Yoghurt Sauce 43
Kale Chips with Sesame and Root Veggie Chips with Herb Salt 43
Goat Cheese-and-Garlic Crostini and Garlic-Roasted Tomatoes and Olives 43
Rumaki and Cheese-Stuffed Blooming Onion 44
Peppery Chicken Meatballs and Pepperoni Pizza Dip 44
Garlicky-and-Cheesy French Fries and Crunchy Basil White Beans 45

Chapter 8 Vegetables and Sides — 46

Breaded Green Tomatoes and Garlic Cauliflower with Tahini 47
Broccoli with Sesame Dressing and Courgette Fritters 47
Courgette Balls-and-Bacon Potatoes and Green Beans 48
Mashed Sweet Potato Tots and Parsnip Fries with Romesco Sauce 48
Rosemary-Roasted Red Potatoes and Crispy Green Beans ... 48
Dijon Roast Cabbage and Scalloped Potatoes 49
Citrus Sweet Potatoes and Carrots and Fried Courgette Salad 49
Golden Pickles and Balsamic Brussels Sprouts 49
Spiced Butternut Squash and Tofu Bites 50
Stuffed Red Peppers with Herbed Ricotta-and-Tomatoes-and-Crispy Garlic Sliced Aubergine 50
Parmesan Herb Focaccia Bread and Roasted Grape Tomatoes-and-Asparagus 50
Easy Potato Croquettes and Super Cheesy Gold Aubergine 51
Fried Brussels Sprouts and Southwestern Roasted Corn 51
Spicy Roasted Bok Choy and Maple-Roasted Tomatoes 52
Spinach-and-Cheese Stuffed Tomatoes and Simple Cougette Crisps 52

Chapter 9 Vegetarian Mains — 53

Cauliflower, Chickpea, and Avocado Mash and Air Fryer Veggies with Halloumi 54
Baked Turnip-and-Courgette and Courgette-and-Spinach Croquettes 54
Caprese Aubergine Stacks and Cheese Stuffed Courgette 54
Italian Baked Egg and Veggies and Pesto Spinach Flatbread 55
Mushroom and Pepper Pizza Squares 55
Garlic White Courgette Rolls and Crispy Tofu 55
Cheesy Cauliflower Pizza Crust and Broccoli-Cheese Fritters 56
Loaded Cauliflower Steak and Aubergine and Courgette Bites 56

Chapter 10 Desserts — 57

Cinnamon Cupcakes with Cream Cheese Frosting and Zucchini Bread 58
Brown Sugar Banana Bread and Hazelnut Butter Cookies 58
Coconut Mixed Berry Crisp and Peanut Butter, Honey & Banana Toast 59
Blackberry Peach Cobbler with Vanilla and Honeyed, Roasted Apples with Walnuts 59
Mini Peanut Butter Tarts 59
Coconut-Custard Pie and Pears with Honey-Lemon Ricotta 60
Glazed Cherry Turnovers 60
Almond Shortbread and Crispy Pineapple Rings 60
Chocolate and Rum Cupcakes and Air Fryer Apple Fritters 61
Indian Toast-and-Milk and Rhubarb-and-Strawberry Crumble 61
Strawberry Shortcake and Crumbly Coconut-Pecan Cookies 62

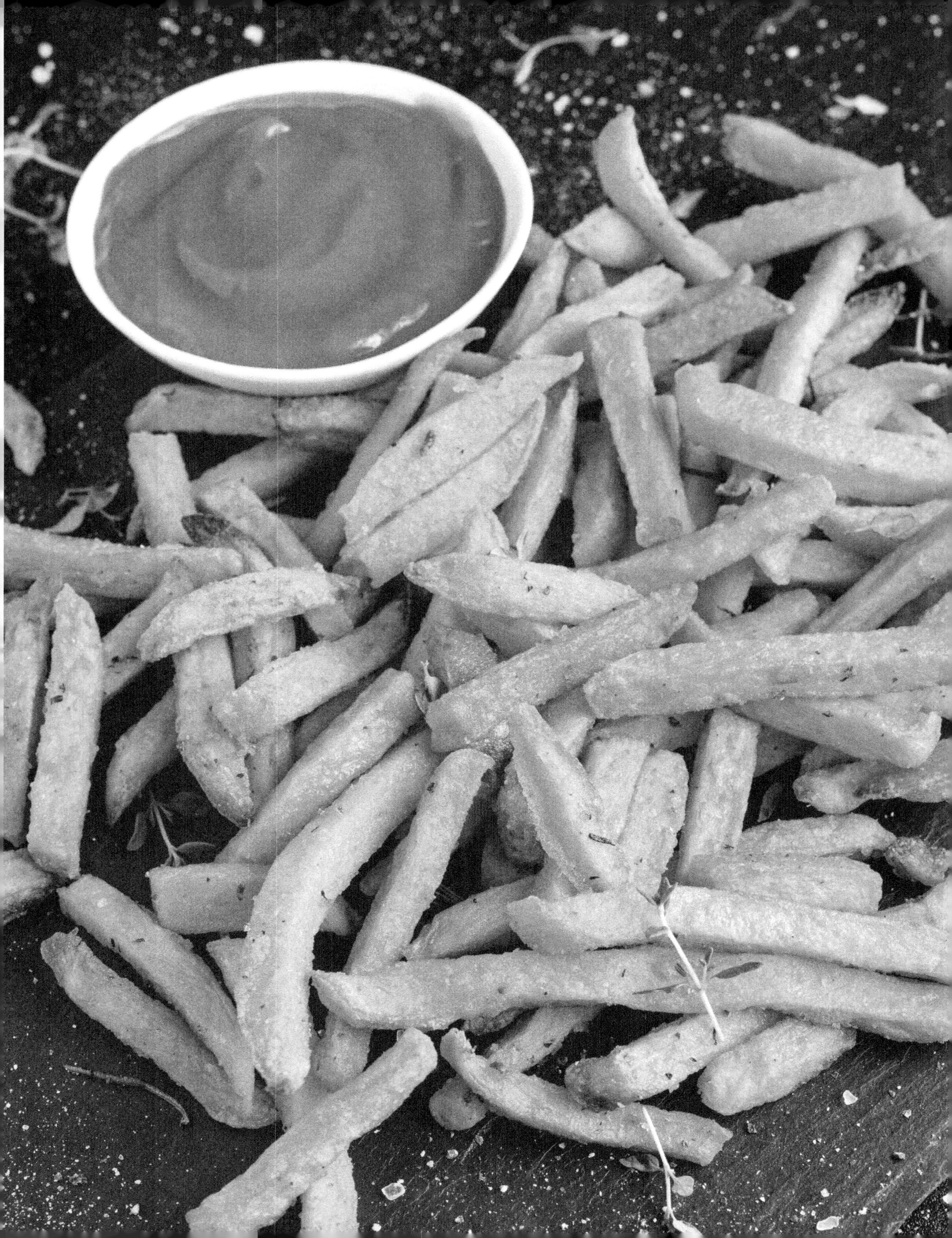

INTRODUCTION

Do you love the taste of fried foods but hate the negative health effects? The Ninja Dual Zone Air Fryer Cookbook is here to revolutionize the way you cook and enjoy your favourite foods. With this cookbook, you can enjoy crispy, flavourful meals without the guilt and without sacrificing taste.

The Ninja Dual Zone Air Fryer has quickly become a household name in the world of cooking, and for good reason. Its advanced dual zone cooking technology allows you to cook two different dishes at the same time, saving you time and hassle in the kitchen. And with its hot air cooking technology, you can achieve that perfect crispy texture without using any unhealthy oils.

This cookbook is your go-to guide for making delicious meals in your Ninja Dual Zone Air Fryer. Whether you're new to the world of air frying or a seasoned pro, you'll find something to love in these recipes. From breakfast to dinner to snacks and desserts, this cookbook has it all.

Each recipe is meticulously crafted to ensure that you get the perfect results every time. The recipes are easy to follow and include step-by-step instructions that make cooking a breeze. And with a list of readily available ingredients, you can quickly and easily prepare delicious meals without having to search for hard-to-find ingredients.

One of the best things about the Ninja Dual Zone Air Fryer is that it allows you to enjoy your favourite foods without the added calories and fat of traditional frying methods. With this cookbook, you'll be able to cook up healthier versions of your favourite meals, like crispy fried chicken, savoury fries, and even sweet treats like doughnuts and muffins.

But healthy doesn't have to mean bland or boring. The recipes in this cookbook are bursting with flavour and will satisfy even the pickiest eaters. From juicy meats to crispy veggies, you'll find something to love in every recipe.

Cooking with the Ninja Dual Zone Air Fryer is not only healthier but also more convenient. With its dual zone cooking technology, you can prepare multiple dishes at once, making mealtime a breeze. And with its fast cooking times, you can have a delicious, homemade meal on the table in no time.

So whether you're looking to cook up healthier versions of your favourite foods or try out some new and exciting recipes, the Ninja Dual Zone Air Fryer Cookbook has got you covered. With its easy-to-follow recipes and step-by-step instructions, you'll be cooking up a storm in no time. So why wait? Grab your copy today and start enjoying the delicious, crispy meals you love without the guilt!

Chapter 1 Breakfasts

Chapter 1 Breakfasts

Egg Tarts and Mushroom-and-Tomato Stuffed Hash Browns

Prep time: 20 minutes | Cook time: 20 minutes

Egg Tart| Serves 2:
⅓ sheet frozen puff pastry, thawed
Cooking oil spray
120 ml shredded Cheddar cheese
2 eggs
¼ teaspoon salt, divided
1 teaspoon minced fresh parsley (optional)
Tomato Stuffed Hash Browns| Serves 4:
Olive oil cooking spray
1 tablespoon plus 2 teaspoons olive oil, divided
110 g baby mushrooms, diced
1 spring onion, white parts and green parts, diced
1 garlic clove, minced
475 ml shredded potatoes
½ teaspoon salt
¼ teaspoon black pepper
1 plum tomato, diced
120 ml shredded mozzarella

1. Insert the crisper plate into the basket and the basket into the unit. Preheat the zone 1 by selecting BAKE, setting the temperature to 180°C. setting the time to 3 minutes. Select START to begin. 2. Lay the puff pastry sheet on a piece of parchment paper and cut it in half. 3. Once the unit is preheated, spray the crisper plate with cooking oil. Transfer the 2 squares of pastry to the basket, keeping them on the parchment paper. 4. Lightly coat the inside of a 6-inch cake pan with olive oil cooking spray. 5. In a small skillet, heat 2 teaspoons olive oil over medium heat. Add the mushrooms, spring onion, and garlic, and cook for 4 to 5 minutes, or until they have softened and are beginning to show some color. Remove from heat. 6. Meanwhile, in a large bowl, combine the potatoes, salt, pepper, and the remaining tablespoon olive oil. Toss until all potatoes are well coated. 7. Pour half of the potatoes into the bottom of the cake pan. Top with the mushroom mixture, tomato, and mozzarella. Spread the remaining potatoes over the top. 8. Set the temperature to 200°C, and set the time to 20 minutes in the zone 1 and 12 to 15 minutes in the zone 2. Select BAKE. Select START to begin, or until the top is golden brown. 9. After 10 minutes, use a metal spoon to press down the center of each pastry square to make a well. Divide the cheese equally between the baked pastries. Carefully crack an egg on top of the cheese, and sprinkle each with the salt. Resume cooking for 7 to 10 minutes. 10. When the cooking is complete, the eggs will be cooked through. Sprinkle each with parsley (if using) and serve. 11. Remove from the zone 2 and allow to cool for 5 minutes before slicing and serving.

Broccoli-Mushroom Frittata and Sausage Stuffed Peppers

Prep time: 25 minutes | Cook time: 20 minutes

Broccoli-Mushroom Frittata| Serves 2:
1 tablespoon olive oil
350 ml broccoli florets, finely chopped
120 ml sliced brown mushrooms
60 ml finely chopped onion
½ teaspoon salt
¼ teaspoon freshly ground black pepper
6 eggs
60 ml Parmesan cheese
Sausage Stuffed Peppers| Serves 4:
230 g spicy pork sausage meat, removed from casings
4 large eggs
110 g full-fat cream cheese, softened
60 ml tinned diced tomatoes, drained
4 green peppers
8 tablespoons shredded chilli cheese
120 ml full-fat sour cream

1. In a nonstick cake pan, combine the olive oil, broccoli, mushrooms, onion, salt, and pepper. Stir until the vegetables are thoroughly coated with oil. Place the cake pan in the air fryer basket and set the air fryer to 200°C. Air fry for 5 minutes until the vegetables soften. 2. Meanwhile, in a medium bowl, whisk the eggs and Parmesan until thoroughly combined. Pour the egg mixture into the pan and shake gently to distribute the vegetables in the zone 1. 3. In a medium skillet over medium heat, crumble and brown the sausage meat until no pink remains. Remove sausage and drain the fat from the pan. Crack eggs into the pan, scramble, and cook until no longer runny. 4. Place cooked sausage in a large bowl and fold in cream cheese. Mix in diced tomatoes. Gently fold in eggs. 5. Cut a 4-inch to 5-inch slit in the top of each pepper, removing the seeds and white membrane with a small knife. Separate the filling into four servings and spoon carefully into each pepper. Top each with 2 tablespoons cheese. 6. Place each pepper into the zone 2. 6. Set the temperature to 180°C. Set the time to 15 minutes. Select MATCH COOK. Select START. 7. Remove from the air fryer and let sit for 5 minutes to cool slightly. Use a silicone spatula to gently lift the frittata onto a plate before serving. 8. 9. Peppers will be soft and cheese will be browned when ready. Serve immediately with sour cream on top.

Canadian Bacon Muffin Sandwiches and Egg-and-Bacon Muffins

Prep time: 10 minutes | Cook time: 15 minutes

Canadian Bacon Muffin Sandwiches| Serves 4:
4 English muffins, split
8 slices back bacon
4 slices cheese
Cooking spray
Egg-and-Bacon Muffins| Serves 1:
2 eggs
Salt and ground black pepper, to taste
1 tablespoon green pesto
85 g shredded Cheddar cheese
140 g cooked bacon
1 spring onion, chopped

1. Preheat the air fryer to 180℃. 2. Make the sandwiches: Top each of 4 muffin halves with 2 slices of bacon, 1 slice of cheese, and finish with the remaining muffin half. 3. Line a cupcake tin with parchment paper. 4. Beat the eggs with pepper, salt, and pesto in a bowl. Mix in the cheese. 5. Pour the eggs into the cupcake tin and top with the bacon and spring onion. 6. Put the sandwiches in the zone 1 and spritz the tops with cooking spray. 7. Set the temperature to 200℃. Set the time to 4 minutes for the zone 1 and 15 minutes for the zone 2. Select Bake. Select START. Flip the sandwiches and bake for another 4 minutes, or until the egg is set. 8. Serve immediately. Divide the sandwiches among four plates and serve warm.

Savory Sweet Potato Hash and Spinach-and-Mushroom Mini Quiche

Prep time: 25 minutes | Cook time: 18 minutes

Savory Sweet Potato Hash | Serves 6 :
2 medium sweet potatoes, peeled and cut into 1-inch cubes
½ green pepper, diced
½ red onion, diced
110 g baby mushrooms, diced
2 tablespoons olive oil
1 garlic clove, minced
½ teaspoon salt
½ teaspoon black pepper
½ tablespoon chopped fresh rosemary
Mushroom Mini Quiche| Serves 4:
1 teaspoon olive oil, plus more for spraying
235 ml coarsely chopped mushrooms
235 ml fresh baby spinach, shredded
4 eggs, beaten
120 ml shredded Cheddar cheese
120 ml shredded Mozzarella cheese
¼ teaspoon salt
¼ teaspoon black pepper

1. Preheat the air fryer to 180℃. 2. In a large bowl, toss all ingredients together until the vegetables are well coated and seasonings distributed. 3. In a medium sauté pan over medium heat, warm 1 teaspoon of olive oil. Add the mushrooms and sauté until soft, 3 to 4 minutes. 4. Add the spinach and cook until wilted, 1 to 2 minutes. Set aside. 5. In a medium bowl, whisk together the eggs, Cheddar cheese, Mozzarella cheese, salt, and pepper. 9. Gently fold the mushrooms and spinach into the egg mixture. 6. Pour the vegetables into the zone 1, making sure they are in a single even layer. (If using a smaller air fryer, you may need to do this in two batches.) 7. Spray 4 silicone baking cups with olive oil and set aside. 8. Pour ¼ of the mixture into each silicone baking cup. Place the baking cups into the zone 2. 8. Set the temperature to 180℃. Set the time to 9 minutes for the zone 1 and 5 minutes for the zone 2. Select Roast for the zone 1 and AIE FRY foe the zone 2. Select START, then toss or flip the vegetables. Roast for 9 minutes more. 9. Stir the mixture in each ramekin slightly and air fry until the egg has set, an additional 3 to 5 minutes. 11. Transfer to a serving bowl or individual plates and enjoy.

Breakfast Sausage and Cauliflower and Nutty Granola

Prep time: 10 minutes | Cook time: 1 hour | Serves 4

Breakfast Sausage and Cauliflower:
450 g sausage meat, cooked and crumbled
475 ml double/whipping cream
1 head cauliflower, chopped
235 ml grated Cheddar cheese, plus more for topping
8 eggs, beaten
Salt and ground black pepper, to taste
Nutty Granola:
120 ml pecans, coarsely chopped
120 ml walnuts or almonds, coarsely chopped
60 ml desiccated coconut
60 ml almond flour
60 ml ground flaxseed or chia seeds
2 tablespoons sunflower seeds
2 tablespoons melted butter
60 ml granulated sweetener
½ teaspoon ground cinnamon
½ teaspoon vanilla extract
¼ teaspoon ground nutmeg
¼ teaspoon salt
2 tablespoons water

1.Preheat the air fryer to 180℃. 2. In a large bowl, mix the sausage, cream, chopped cauliflower, cheese and eggs. Sprinkle with salt and ground black pepper. 3. Cut a piece of parchment paper to fit inside the zone 1. 4. In a large bowl, toss the nuts, coconut, almond flour, ground flaxseed or chia seeds, sunflower seeds, butter, sweetener, cinnamon, vanilla, nutmeg, salt, and water until thoroughly combined. 5. Spread the granola on the parchment paper and flatten to an even thickness. 6. Pour the mixture into a greased casserole dish. Set the temperature to 180℃. Set the time to 45 minutes and BAKE for the zone 1. Set the time to an hour and AIR FRY for the zone 2. Seclect START. 7. Remove from the air fryer and allow to fully cool. Break the granola into bite-size pieces and store in a covered container for up to a week. 8. Top with more Cheddar cheese and serve.

Egg in a Hole and Chimichanga Breakfast Burrito

Prep time: 15 minutes | Cook time: 10 minutes

Egg in a Hole | Serves 1:	tortillas
1 slice bread	120 ml canned refried beans
1 teaspoon butter, softened	(pinto or black work equally
1 egg	well)
Salt and pepper, to taste	4 large eggs, cooked scrambled
1 tablespoon shredded Cheddar	4 corn tortilla chips, crushed
cheese	120 ml grated chili cheese
2 teaspoons diced ham	12 pickled jalapeño slices
Chimichanga Breakfast Burrito|	1 tablespoon vegetable oil
Serves 2:	Guacamole, salsa, and sour
2 large (10- to 12-inch) flour	cream, for serving (optional)

1. Preheat the air fryer to 180°C. Place a baking dish in the zone 1. 2. On a flat work surface, cut a hole in the center of the bread slice with a 2½-inch-diameter biscuit cutter. 3. Spread the butter evenly on each side of the bread slice and transfer to the baking dish. 4. Crack the egg into the hole and season as desired with salt and pepper. Scatter the shredded cheese and diced ham on top. 5. Place the tortillas on a work surface and divide the refried beans between them, spreading them in a rough rectangle in the center of the tortillas. Top the beans with the scrambled eggs, crushed chips, cheese, and jalapeños. Fold one side over the fillings, then fold in each short side and roll up the rest of the way like a burrito. 6. Brush the outside of the burritos with the oil, then transfer to the zone 2, seam-side down. 7. Set the temperature to 180°C. Set the time to 10 minutes. Select AIR FRY. Select START. Until the tortillas are browned and crisp and the filling is warm throughout. 8. Select Bake for the zone 2 for 5 minutes until the bread is lightly browned and the egg is cooked to your preference. 9. Transfer the chimichangas to plates and serve warm with guacamole, salsa, and sour cream, if you like. 10. Remove from the basket and serve hot.

Oat-and-Chia Porridge and Pizza Eggs

Prep time: 15 minutes | Cook time: 10 minutes

Oat and Chia Porridge| Serves 4:	235 ml shredded Mozzarella cheese
2 tablespoons peanut butter	7 slices pepperoni, chopped
4 tablespoons honey	1 large egg, whisked
1 tablespoon butter, melted	¼ teaspoon dried oregano
1 L milk	¼ teaspoon dried parsley
475 ml oats	¼ teaspoon garlic powder
235 ml chia seeds	¼ teaspoon salt
Pizza Eggs| Serves 2:	

1. Preheat the air fryer to 180°C. 2. Put the peanut butter, honey, butter, and milk in a bowl and stir to mix. Add the oats and chia seeds and stir. 3. Place Mozzarella in a single layer on the bottom of an ungreased round nonstick baking dish. Scatter pepperoni over cheese, then pour egg evenly around baking dish. 4. Transfer the mixture to a bowl in the zone 1. Sprinkle with remaining ingredients and place into zone 2. 5. Set the temperature to 180°C and the time to 5 minutes for the zone 1. Set the temperature to 170°C and the time to 10 minutes for the zone 2. Select BAKE. Select START. When cheese is brown and egg is set, dish will be done. 6. Let cool in dish 5 minutes before serving.

Lemon-Blueberry Muffins and Wholemeal Banana-Walnut Bread

Prep time: 15 minutes | Cook time: 23 minutes | Serves 6

Lemon-Blueberry Muffins:	2 ripe medium bananas
300 ml almond flour	1 large egg
3 tablespoons granulated sweetener	60 ml non-fat plain Greek yoghurt
1 teaspoon baking powder	60 ml olive oil
2 large eggs	½ teaspoon vanilla extract
3 tablespoons melted butter	2 tablespoons honey
1 tablespoon almond milk	235 ml wholemeal flour
1 tablespoon fresh lemon juice	¼ teaspoon salt
120 ml fresh blueberries	¼ teaspoon baking soda
Wholemeal Banana-Walnut Bread:	½ teaspoon ground cinnamon
	60 ml chopped walnuts
Olive oil cooking spray	

1. Preheat the air fryer to 180°C. Lightly coat 6 silicone muffin cups with vegetable oil. Set aside. 2. In a large mixing bowl, combine the almond flour, sweetener, and baking soda. Set aside. 3. In a separate small bowl, whisk together the eggs, butter, milk, and lemon juice. Add the egg mixture to the flour mixture and stir until just combined. Fold in the blueberries and let the batter sit for 5 minutes. 4. Spoon the muffin batter into the muffin cups, about two-thirds full. 5. Lightly coat the inside of a 8-by-4-inch loaf pan with olive oil cooking spray. (Or use two 5 ½-by-3-inch loaf pans.) 6. In a large bowl, mash the bananas with a fork. Add the egg, yoghurt, olive oil, vanilla, and honey. Mix until well combined and mostly smooth. 7. Sift the wholemeal flour, salt, baking soda, and cinnamon into the wet mixture, then stir until just combined. Do not overmix. 8. Gently fold in the walnuts. 9. Pour into the prepared loaf pan and spread to distribute evenly. 10. Put the muffins in the zone 1, select AIR FRY. Place the loaf pan in the zone 2 and select BAKE, setting the time to 23 minutes the temperature to 200°C. Select MATCH COOK. Select START. Until golden brown on top and a toothpick inserted into the center comes out clean. 11. Allow to cool for 5 minutes before serving.

Banana-Nut Muffins

Prep time: 5 minutes | Cook time: 15 minutes | Makes 10 muffins

Oil, for spraying	1 large egg
2 very ripe bananas	1 teaspoon vanilla extract
120 ml packed light brown sugar	180 ml plain flour
	1 teaspoon baking powder
80 ml rapeseed oil or vegetable oil	1 teaspoon ground cinnamon
	120 ml chopped walnuts

1. Preheat the air fryer to 180°C. Spray 10 silicone muffin cups lightly with oil. 2. In a medium bowl, mash the bananas. Add the brown sugar, rapeseed oil, egg, and vanilla and stir to combine. 3. Fold in the flour, baking powder, and cinnamon until just combined. 4. Add the walnuts and fold a few times to distribute throughout the batter. 5. Divide the batter equally among the prepared muffin cups and place them in the dual zone. You may need to work in batches, depending on the size of your air fryer. 6. Set the temperature to 200°C. Cook for 15 minutes, or until golden brown and a toothpick inserted into the center of a muffin comes out clean. Select AIR FRY. SELECT START. 7. The air fryer tends to brown muffins more than the oven, so don't be alarmed if they are darker than you're used to. They will still taste great. 8. Let cool on a wire rack before serving.

Jalapeño-and-Bacon Breakfast Pizza and Denver Omelette

Prep time: 10 minutes | Cook time: 10 minutes

Jalapeño and Bacon Breakfast Pizza| Serves 2:	¼ teaspoon fine sea salt
	⅛ teaspoon ground black pepper
235 ml shredded Mozzarella cheese	60 ml diced ham (omit for vegetarian)
30 g cream cheese, broken into small pieces	60 ml diced green and red peppers
4 slices cooked bacon, chopped	2 tablespoons diced spring onions, plus more for garnish
60 ml chopped pickled jalapeños	60 ml shredded Cheddar cheese (about 30 g) (omit for dairy-free)
1 large egg, whisked	
¼ teaspoon salt	
Denver Omelette| Serves 1:	Quartered cherry tomatoes, for serving (optional)
2 large eggs	
60 ml unsweetened, unflavoured almond milk	

1. Preheat the air fryer to 180°C. Grease a cake pan and set aside. Place Mozzarella in a single layer on the bottom of an ungreased round nonstick baking dish. Scatter cream cheese pieces, bacon, and jalapeños over Mozzarella, then pour egg evenly around baking dish. 2. In a small bowl, use a fork to whisk together the eggs, almond milk, salt, and pepper. Add the ham, peppers, and spring onions. Pour the mixture into the greased pan. Add the cheese on top (if using). 3. Sprinkle with salt and place into zone 1. Place the pan in the zone 2 of the air fryer. 4. Adjust the temperature to 170°C. Set the time to 10 minutes for the zone 1 and 8 minutes for the zone 2. Select BAKE. Select START. When cheese is brown and egg is set, pizza will be done, and until the eggs are cooked to your liking. 7. Loosen the omelette from the sides of the pan with a spatula and place it on a serving plate. Garnish with spring onions and serve with cherry tomatoes, if desired. Best served fresh.

Breakfast Meatballs and Cauliflower Avocado Toast

Prep time: 25 minutes | Cook time: 15 minutes

Breakfast Meatballs|Makes 18 meatballs:	Cauliflower Avocado Toast| Serves 2:
450 g pork sausage meat, removed from casings	1 (40 g) steamer bag cauliflower
½ teaspoon salt	1 large egg
¼ teaspoon ground black pepper	120 ml shredded Mozzarella cheese
120 ml shredded sharp Cheddar cheese	1 ripe medium avocado
	½ teaspoon garlic powder
30 g cream cheese, softened	¼ teaspoon ground black pepper
1 large egg, whisked	

1. Combine all ingredients in a large bowl. Form mixture into eighteen 1-inch meatballs. 2. Cook cauliflower according to package instructions. Remove from bag and place into cheesecloth or clean towel to remove excess moisture. Place meatballs into ungreased zone 1. 3. Place cauliflower into a large bowl and mix in egg and Mozzarella. Cut a piece of parchment to fit your air fryer basket. Separate the cauliflower mixture into two, and place it on the parchment in two mounds. 4. Press out the cauliflower mounds into a ¼-inch-thick rectangle. Place the parchment into the zone 2. 5. Set the temperature to 200°C. Set the time to 15 minutes for the zone 1 and 8 minutes for the zone 2. Select AIR FRY. Select START. Shaking basket three times during cooking. 6. When the timer beeps, remove the parchment and allow the cauliflower to cool 5 minutes. 7. Cut open the avocado and remove the pit. Scoop out the inside, place it in a medium bowl, and mash it with garlic powder and pepper. Spread onto the cauliflower. Flip the cauliflower halfway through the cooking time. 8. Meatballs will be browned on the outside and have an internal temperature of at least 64°C when completely cooked. Serve warm and immediately.

Oat Bran Muffins and Pork Sausage Eggs with Mustard Sauce

Prep time: 30 minutes | Cook time: 12 minutes per batch | Serves 8

Oat Bran Muffins:
160 ml oat bran
120 ml flour
60 ml brown sugar
1 teaspoon baking powder
½ teaspoon baking soda
⅛ teaspoon salt
120 ml buttermilk
1 egg
2 tablespoons rapeseed oil
120 ml chopped dates, raisins, or dried cranberries
24 paper muffin cups
Cooking spray

Pork Sausage Eggs with Mustard Sauce:
450 g pork sausage meat
8 soft-boiled or hard-boiled eggs, peeled
1 large egg
2 tablespoons milk
235 ml crushed pork scratchings
Smoky Mustard Sauce:
60 ml mayonnaise
2 tablespoons sour cream
1 tablespoon Dijon mustard
1 teaspoon chipotle hot sauce

1. Preheat the air fryer to 180°C. 2. In a large bowl, combine the oat bran, flour, brown sugar, baking powder, baking soda, and salt. 3. In a small bowl, beat together the buttermilk, egg, and oil. 4. Pour buttermilk mixture into bowl with dry ingredients and stir just until moistened. Do not beat. 5. Gently stir in dried fruit. 6. Use triple baking cups to help muffins hold shape during baking. Spray them with cooking spray, place 8 sets of cups in the zone 1, and fill each one ¾ full of batter. 6. Divide the sausage into 8 portions. Take each portion of sausage, pat it down into a patty, and place 1 egg in the middle, gently wrapping the sausage around the egg until the egg is completely covered. (Wet your hands slightly if you find the sausage to be too sticky.) Repeat with the remaining eggs and sausage. 7. In a small shallow bowl, whisk the egg and milk until frothy. In another shallow bowl, place the crushed pork scratchings. Working one at a time, dip a sausage-wrapped egg into the beaten egg and then into the pork scratchings, gently rolling to coat evenly. Repeat with the remaining sausage-wrapped eggs. 8. Arrange the eggs in the zone 2, and lightly spray with olive oil. 9. Set the temperature to 200°C. Set the time to 10 to 12 minutes and select BAKE, until top springs back when lightly touched and toothpick inserted in center comes out clean. Select MATCH COOK. Select START. 10. Repeat for remaining muffins, pausing halfway through the baking time to turn the eggs, until the eggs are hot and the sausage is cooked through. 11. To make the sauce: In a small bowl, combine the mayonnaise, sour cream, Dijon, and hot sauce. Whisk until thoroughly combined. Serve with the Scotch eggs.

Honey-Apricot Granola with Greek Yoghurt and Egg White Cups

Prep time: 20 minutes | Cook time: 30 minutes

Honey-Apricot Granola with Greek Yoghurt| Serves 6:
235 ml rolled oats
60 ml dried apricots, diced
60 ml almond slivers
60 ml walnuts, chopped
60 ml pumpkin seeds
60 to 80 ml honey, plus more for drizzling
1 tablespoon olive oil
1 teaspoon ground cinnamon
¼ teaspoon ground nutmeg
¼ teaspoon salt
2 tablespoons sugar-free dark chocolate chips (optional)
700 ml fat-free plain Greek yoghurt
Egg White Cups| Serves 4
475 ml 100% liquid egg whites
3 tablespoons salted butter, melted
¼ teaspoon salt
¼ teaspoon onion granules
½ medium plum tomato, cored and diced
120 ml chopped fresh spinach leaves

1. Preheat the air fryer to 180°C. Line the zone 1 with parchment paper. 2. In a large bowl, combine the oats, apricots, almonds, walnuts, pumpkin seeds, honey, olive oil, cinnamon, nutmeg, and salt, mixing so that the honey, oil, and spices are well distributed. 3. In a large bowl, whisk egg whites with butter, salt, and onion granules. Stir in tomato and spinach, then pour evenly into four ramekins greased with cooking spray. 4. Devide the mixture two portions and pour the mixture onto the parchment paper in the zone 1 and spread it into an even layer. Place ramekins into zone 2. 5. Set the temperature to 150°C. Set the time to 10 minutes in the zone 1 and 15 minutes in the zone 2. Select Bake. Select START, then shake or stir and spread back out into an even layer. Continue baking for 10 minutes more, then repeat the process of shaking or stirring the mixture. Bake for an additional 10 minutes before removing from the air fryer. 6. For each serving, top 120 ml Greek yoghurt with 80 ml granola and a drizzle of honey, if needed. Eggs will be fully cooked and firm in the center when done. Serve warm. 7. Allow the granola to cool completely before stirring in the chocolate chips (if using) and pouring into an airtight container for storage.

Cinnamon-Raisin Bagels and Scotch Eggs

Prep time: 40 minutes | Cook time: 20 minutes | Serves 4

Cinnamon-Raisin Bagels:
Oil, for spraying
60 ml raisins
235 ml self-raising flour, plus more for dusting
235 ml plain Greek yoghurt
1 teaspoon ground cinnamon
1 large egg
Scotch Eggs:
2 tablespoons flour, plus extra for coating
450 g sausage meat
4 hard-boiled eggs, peeled
1 raw egg
1 tablespoon water
Oil for misting or cooking spray
Crumb Coating:
180 ml panko bread crumbs
180 ml flour

1. Combine flour with sausage meat and mix thoroughly. 2. Divide into 4 equal portions and mold each around a hard-boiled egg so the sausage completely covers the egg. 3. In a small bowl, beat together the raw egg and water. 4. Dip sausage-covered eggs in the remaining flour, then the egg mixture, then roll in the crumb coating. 5. In a large bowl, mix together the flour, yoghurt, and cinnamon with your hands or a large silicone spatula until a ball is formed. It will be quite sticky for a while. 6. Drain the raisins and gently work them into the ball of dough. 7. Place the dough on a lightly floured work surface and divide into 4 equal pieces. Roll each piece into an 8- or 9-inch-long rope and shape it into a circle, pinching the ends together to seal. Place the dough in the zone 1. 8. In a small bowl, whisk the egg. Brush the egg onto the tops of the dough. Line the zone 2 with parchment and spray lightly with oil. Place the dough in the zone 2. 9. Place the raisins in a bowl of hot water and let sit for 10 to 15 minutes, until they have plumped. This will make them extra juicy. 10. Set the temperature to 180ºC. Set the time to 10 minutes. Select MATCH COOK. Select START. Spray eggs, turn, and spray other side in the zone 2. 6. Continue cooking for another 10 to 15 minutes or until sausage is well done. 7. 8. Serve immediately.

Golden Avocado Tempura and Turkey Breakfast Sausage Patties

Prep time: 10 minutes | Cook time: 10 minutes | Serves 4

Golden Avocado Tempura:
120 ml bread crumbs
½ teaspoons salt
1 Haas avocado, pitted, peeled and sliced
Liquid from 1 can white beans
Turkey Breakfast Sausage Patties:
1 tablespoon chopped fresh thyme
1 tablespoon chopped fresh sage
1¼ teaspoons coarse or flaky salt
1 teaspoon chopped fennel seeds
¾ teaspoon smoked paprika
½ teaspoon onion granules
½ teaspoon garlic powder
⅛ teaspoon crushed red pepper flakes
⅛ teaspoon freshly ground black pepper
450 g lean turkey mince
120 ml finely minced sweet apple (peeled)

1. Preheat the air fryer to 180ºC. 2. Mix the bread crumbs and salt in a shallow bowl until well-incorporated. 3. Dip the avocado slices in the bean liquid, then into the bread crumbs. 4. Thoroughly combine the thyme, sage, salt, fennel seeds, paprika, onion granules, garlic powder, red pepper flakes, and black pepper in a medium bowl. 5. Add the turkey mince and apple and stir until well incorporated. Divide the mixture into 8 equal portions and shape into patties with your hands, each about ¼ inch thick and 3 inches in diameter. 6. Put the avocados in the zone 1, taking care not to overlap any slices. Place the patties in a single layer in the zone 2. You may need to work in batches to avoid overcrowding. 7. Set the temperature to 200ºC, and setting the time to 5 minutes for the zone 1 and 10 minutes for the zone 2, giving the zone 1 a good shake at the halfway point. Select AIR FRY. Select START. Flip the patties and air fry for 5 minutes, or until the patties are nicely browned and cooked through. 8. Remove from the basket to a plate and repeat with the remaining patties. 9. Serve warm and immediately.

Chapter 2 Family Favorites

Chapter 2 Family Favorites

Steak and Vegetable Kebabs and Filo Vegetable Triangles

Prep time: 30 minutes | Cook time: 7 minutes

Steak and Vegetable Kebabs | Serves 4:
2 tablespoons balsamic vinegar
2 teaspoons olive oil
½ teaspoon dried marjoram
⅛ teaspoon freshly ground black pepper
340 g silverside steak, cut into 1-inch pieces
1 red pepper, sliced
16 button mushrooms
235 ml cherry tomatoes
Filo Vegetable Triangles| Serves 6:
3 tablespoons minced onion
2 garlic cloves, minced
2 tablespoons grated carrot
1 teaspoon olive oil
3 tablespoons frozen baby peas, thawed
2 tablespoons fat-free soft white cheese, at room temperature
6 sheets frozen filo pastry, thawed
Olive oil spray, for coating the dough

1.In a medium bowl, stir together the balsamic vinegar, olive oil, marjoram, and black pepper. 2. Add the steak and stir to coat. Let stand for 10 minutes at room temperature. Alternating items, thread the beef, red pepper, mushrooms, and tomatoes onto 8 bamboo or metal skewers that fit in the zone 1. 3. In a baking pan, combine the onion, garlic, carrot, and olive oil. 4. Lay one sheet of filo on a work surface and lightly spray with olive oil spray. Top with another sheet of filo. 5. Repeat with the remaining 4 filo sheets; you'll have 3 stacks with 2 layers each. Cut each stack lengthwise into 4 strips (12 strips total). 6. Place a scant 2 teaspoons of the filling near the bottom of each strip. 7. Bring one corner up over the filling to make a triangle; continue folding the triangles over, as you would fold a flag. Seal the edge with a bit of water. 8. Repeat with the remaining strips and filling. 9. Set the temperature to 200°C. Set the time to 2 to 4 minutes for the zone 1 and 5 to 7 minutes for the zone 2, or until the vegetables are crisp-tender and the beef is browned and reaches at least 64°C on a meat thermometer. Select AIR FRY. Select START. 10. Transfer to a bowl. Stir in the peas and soft white cheese to the vegetable mixture. Let cool while you prepare the dough. Serve immediately.

Coconut Chicken Tenders and Pork Burgers with Red Cabbage Salad

Prep time: 30 minutes | Cook time: 12 minutes | Serves 4

Coconut Chicken Tenders:
Oil, for spraying
2 large eggs
60 ml milk
1 tablespoon hot sauce
350 ml sweetened flaked or desiccated coconut
180 ml panko breadcrumbs
1 teaspoon salt
½ teaspoon freshly ground black pepper
450 g chicken tenders
Pork Burgers with Red Cabbage Salad:
120 ml Greek yoghurt
2 tablespoons low-salt mustard, divided
1 tablespoon lemon juice
60 ml sliced red cabbage
60 ml grated carrots
450 g lean minced pork
½ teaspoon paprika
235 ml mixed baby lettuce greens
2 small tomatoes, sliced
8 small low-salt wholemeal sandwich buns, cut in half

1.Line the zone 1 with parchment and spray lightly with oil. In a small bowl, whisk together the eggs, milk, and hot sauce. 2. In a shallow dish, mix together the coconut, breadcrumbs, salt, and black pepper. 3.Coat the chicken in the egg mix, then dredge in the coconut mixture until evenly coated. 4. In a small bowl, combine the yoghurt, 1 tablespoon mustard, lemon juice, cabbage, and carrots; mix and refrigerate. 5. In a medium bowl, combine the pork, remaining 1 tablespoon mustard, and paprika. Form into 8 small patties. 6. Place the chicken in the zone 1 and spray liberally with oil. Put the sliders into the zone 2. 7. Set the temperature to 200°C Set the time to 6 minutes for the zone 1 and 7 to 9 minutes for the zone 2, flip, spray with more oil, and cook for another 6 minutes in the zone 1, or until the internal temperature reaches 74°C. Until the sliders register 74°C as tested with a meat thermometer. 8. Assemble the burgers by placing some of the lettuce greens on a bun bottom. 9. Top with a tomato slice, the burgers, and the cabbage mixture. Add the bun top and serve immediately.

Chinese-Inspired Spareribs and Fried Green Tomatoes

Prep time: 45 minutes | Cook time: 8 minutes | Serves 4

Chinese-Inspired Spareribs:
Oil, for spraying
340 g boneless pork spareribs, cut into 3-inch-long pieces
235 ml soy sauce
180 ml sugar
120 ml beef or chicken stock
60 ml honey
2 tablespoons minced garlic
1 teaspoon ground ginger
2 drops red food colouring (optional)
Fried Green Tomatoes:
4 medium green tomatoes
80 ml plain flour
2 egg whites
60 ml almond milk
235 ml ground almonds
120 ml panko breadcrumbs
2 teaspoons olive oil
1 teaspoon paprika
1 clove garlic, minced

1. Line the zone 1 with parchment and spray lightly with oil. 2. Combine the ribs, soy sauce, sugar, beef stock, honey, garlic, ginger, and food colouring (if using) in a large zip-top plastic bag, seal, and shake well until completely coated. Refrigerate for at least 30 minutes. 3. Cut the tomatoes into ½-inch slices, discarding the thinner ends. 4. Put the flour on a plate. 5. In a shallow bowl, beat the egg whites with the almond milk until frothy. And on another plate, combine the almonds, breadcrumbs, olive oil, paprika, and garlic and mix well. 6. Dip the tomato slices into the flour, then into the egg white mixture, then into the almond mixture to coat. 7. Place the ribs in the prepared zone 1. Rinse the tomatoes and pat dry. Place four of the coated tomato slices in the zone 2. 8. Set the temperature to 190°C for 8 minutes, or until the internal temperature reaches 74°C. Set the temperature to 200°C for 6 to 8 minutes or until the tomato coating is crisp and golden brown. Select AIR FRY. Select START. Repeat with remaining tomato slices and serve immediately.

Avocado-and-Egg Burrito and Veggie Tuna Melts

Prep time: 25 minutes | Cook time: 11 minutes | Serves 4

Avocado and Egg Burrito:
2 hard-boiled egg whites, chopped
1 hard-boiled egg, chopped
1 avocado, peeled, pitted, and chopped
1 red pepper, chopped
3 tablespoons low-salt salsa, plus additional for serving (optional)
1 (34 g) slice low-salt, low-fat processed cheese, torn into pieces
4 low-salt wholemeal flour tortillas
Veggie Tuna Melts:
2 low-salt wholemeal English muffins, split
1 (170 g) can chunk light low-salt tuna, drained
235 ml shredded carrot
80 ml chopped mushrooms
2 spring onions, white and green parts, sliced
80 ml fat-free Greek yoghurt
2 tablespoons low-salt wholegrain mustard
2 slices low-salt low-fat Swiss cheese, halved

1. In a medium bowl, thoroughly mix the egg whites, egg, avocado, red pepper, salsa, and cheese. 2. Place the tortillas on a work surface and evenly divide the filling among them. 3. Fold in the edges and roll up. Secure the burritos with toothpicks if necessary. 4. In a medium bowl, thoroughly mix the tuna, carrot, mushrooms, spring onions, yoghurt, and mustard. 5. Put the burritos in the zone 1. Top each half of the muffins with one-fourth of the tuna mixture and a half slice of Swiss cheese. Place the English muffin halves in the zone 2. 6. Set the temperature to 200°C for 3 to 5 minutes for the zone 1, or until the burritos are light golden brown and crisp. Serve with more salsa (if using). Set the temperature to 170°C for 4 to 7 minutes for the zone 2, or until the tuna mixture is hot and the cheese melts and starts to brown. Select AIR FRY. Select START. 7. Remove from the basket and set aside. Serve immediately.

Fish-and-Vegetable Tacos and Meatball Subs

Prep time: 30 minutes | Cook time: 19 minutes | Serves 4

Fish-and-Vegetable Tacos:
450 g white fish fillets, such as sole or cod
2 teaspoons olive oil
3 tablespoons freshly squeezed lemon juice, divided
350 ml chopped red cabbage
1 large carrot, grated
120 ml low-salt salsa
80 ml low-fat Greek yoghurt
4 soft low-salt wholemeal tortillas
Meatball Subs | Serves 6:
Oil, for spraying
450 g 15% fat minced beef
120 ml Italian breadcrumbs (mixed breadcrumbs, Italian seasoning and salt)
1 tablespoon dried minced onion
1 tablespoon minced garlic
1 large egg
1 teaspoon salt
1 teaspoon freshly ground black pepper
6 sub rolls
1 (510 g) jar marinara sauce
350 ml shredded Mozzarella cheese

1. Brush the fish with the olive oil and sprinkle with 1 tablespoon of lemon juice. 2. In a medium bowl, stir together the remaining 2 tablespoons of lemon juice, the red cabbage, carrot, salsa, and yoghurt. 3. Oil, for spraying 450 g 15% fat minced beef 120 ml Italian breadcrumbs (mixed breadcrumbs, Italian seasoning and salt) 1 tablespoon dried minced onion 1 tablespoon minced garlic 1 large egg 1 teaspoon salt 1 teaspoon freshly ground black pepper 6 sub rolls 1 (510 g) jar marinara sauce 350 ml shredded Mozzarella cheese. 4. Set the temperature to 200°C. Set the time to 9 to 12 minutes for the zone 1 and 19 minutes for the zone 2. Until the fish just flakes when tested with a fork. Select AIR FRY. Select START. 5. When the fish is cooked, remove it from the air fryer basket and break it up into large pieces. Offer the fish, tortillas, and the cabbage mixture, and let each person assemble a taco.

Chapter 3 Fast and Easy Everyday Favourites

Chapter 3 Fast and Easy Everyday Favourites

Beef Bratwursts and Simple-and-Easy Croutons

Prep time: 10 minutes | Cook time: 15 minutes | Serves 4

Beef Bratwursts:
4 (85 g) beef bratwursts
Simple-and-Easy Croutons:
2 slices bread
1 tablespoon olive oil
Hot soup, for serving

1. Preheat the air fryer to 180°C. 2. Cut the slices of bread into medium-size chunks. 3. Place the beef bratwursts in the zone 1 and brush the zone 2 with the oil. Place the chunks inside. 4. Set the temperature to 200°C. Set the time to 15 minutes for the zone 1 and at least 8 minutes for the zone 2. Select AIR FRY. Select START, turning once halfway through. Serve with hot soup.

Cheesy Chilli Toast and Baked Cheese Sandwich

Prep time: 10 minutes | Cook time: 8 minutes | Serves 1

Cheesy Chilli Toast:
2 tablespoons grated Parmesan cheese
2 tablespoons grated Mozzarella cheese
2 teaspoons salted butter, at room temperature
10 to 15 thin slices serrano chilli or jalapeño
2 slices sourdough bread
½ teaspoon black pepper
Baked Cheese Sandwich|
Serves 2:
2 tablespoons mayonnaise
4 thick slices sourdough bread
4 thick slices Brie cheese
8 slices hot capicola or prosciutto

1. Preheat the air fryer to 180°C. 2. In a small bowl, stir together the Parmesan, Mozzarella, butter, and chillies. 3. Spread half the mixture onto one side of each slice of bread. Sprinkle with the pepper. 4. Spread the mayonnaise on one side of each slice of bread. 5. Place the slices, cheese-side up, in the zone 1. Place 2 slices of bread in the zone 2, mayonnaise-side down. 6. Place the slices of Brie and capicola on the bread and cover with the remaining two slices of bread, mayonnaise-side up. 7. Set the temperature 200°C. Set the time to 5 minutes for the zone 1 and 8 minutes for the zone 2,. Select BAKE. Select START. Until the cheese has melted and started to brown slightly. Serve immediately.

Spinach-and-Carrot Balls and Crunchy Fried Okra

Prep time: 15 minutes | Cook time: 10 minutes | Serves 4

Spinach and Carrot Balls:
2 slices toasted bread
1 carrot, peeled and grated
1 package fresh spinach, blanched and chopped
½ onion, chopped
1 egg, beaten
½ teaspoon garlic powder
1 teaspoon minced garlic
1 teaspoon salt
½ teaspoon black pepper
1 tablespoon Engevita yeast flakes
1 tablespoon flour
Crunchy Fried Okra | Serves 4:
235 ml self-raising yellow cornmeal (alternatively add 1 tablespoon baking powder to cornmeal)
1 teaspoon Italian-style seasoning
1 teaspoon paprika
1 teaspoon salt
½ teaspoon freshly ground black pepper
2 large eggs, beaten
475 ml okra slices
Cooking spray

1. Preheat the air fryer to 180°C. 2. In a food processor, pulse the toasted bread to form breadcrumbs. 3. Transfer into a shallow dish or bowl. In a bowl, mix together all the other ingredients. 4. Use your hands to shape the mixture into small-sized balls. 5. In a shallow bowl, whisk the cornmeal, Italian-style seasoning, paprika, salt, and pepper until blended. 6. Place the beaten eggs in a second shallow bowl. 7. Add the okra to the beaten egg and stir to coat. Add the egg and okra mixture to the cornmeal mixture and stir until coated. 8. Roll the balls in the breadcrumbs, ensuring to cover them well. Put them in the zone 1 and Line the air fryer basket with parchment paper. Place the okra on the parchment in the zone 2 and spritz it with oil. 8. Set the temperature to 200°C. Set the time to 10 minutes for the zone 1 and 4 minutes for the zone 2. Select AIR FRY. Select START. 9. Shake the basket, spritz the okra with oil, and air fry for 4 to 6 minutes more until lightly browned and crispy. Serve immediately.

Buttery Sweet Potatoes and Bacon Pinwheels

Prep time: 15 minutes | Cook time: 10 minutes

Buttery Sweet Potatoes| Serves 4:
- 2 tablespoons butter, melted
- 1 tablespoon light brown sugar
- 2 sweet potatoes, peeled and cut into ½-inch cubes
- Cooking spray

Bacon Pinwheels | Serves 8:
- 1 sheet puff pastry
- 2 tablespoons maple syrup
- 60 ml brown sugar
- 8 slices bacon
- Ground black pepper, to taste
- Cooking spray

1. Preheat the air fryer to 180°C. 2. Line the zone 1 with parchment paper. In a medium bowl, stir together the melted butter and brown sugar until blended. Toss the sweet potatoes in the butter mixture until coated. 3. Spritz the zone 2 with cooking spray. Roll the puff pastry into a 10-inch square with a rolling pin on a clean work surface, then cut the pastry into 8 strips. 4. Brush the strips with maple syrup and sprinkle with sugar, leaving a 1-inch far end uncovered. 5. Arrange each slice of bacon on each strip, leaving a ⅛-inch length of bacon hang over the end close to you. 6. Sprinkle with black pepper. From the end close to you, roll the strips into pinwheels, then dab the uncovered end with water and seal the rolls. 7. Place the sweet potatoes on the parchment and spritz with oil. Arrange the pinwheels in the preheated zone 2 and spritz with cooking spray. 8. Set the temperature to 200°C. Set the time to 5 minutes for the zone 1 and 10 minutes for the zone 2. Select AIR FRY. Select START. 9. Shake the basket, spritz the sweet potatoes with oil, and air fry for 5 minutes more until they're soft enough to cut with a fork. Until golden brown. Flip the pinwheels halfway through. Serve immediately.

Herb-Roasted Veggies and Cheesy Jalapeño Cornbread

Prep time: 10 minutes | Cook time: 20 minutes | Serves 4

- 1 red pepper, sliced
- 1 (230 g) package sliced mushrooms
- 235 ml green beans, cut into 2-inch pieces
- 80 ml diced red onion
- 3 garlic cloves, sliced
- 1 teaspoon olive oil
- ½ teaspoon dried basil
- ½ teaspoon dried tarragon
- Cheesy Jalapeño Cornbread:
- 160 ml cornmeal
- 80 ml plain flour
- ¾ teaspoon baking powder
- 2 tablespoons margarine, melted
- ½ teaspoon rock salt
- 1 tablespoon granulated sugar
- 180 ml whole milk
- 1 large egg, beaten
- 1 jalapeño pepper, thinly sliced
- 80 ml shredded extra mature Cheddar cheese

1. Preheat the air fryer to 180°C. 2. In a medium bowl, mix the red pepper, mushrooms, green beans, red onion, and garlic. 3. Drizzle with the olive oil. Toss to coat. Add the herbs and toss again. Cooking spray. Spritz the air fryer basket with cooking spray. 5. Place the vegetables in the zone 1. 6. Combine all the ingredients in a large bowl. Stir to mix well. Pour the mixture in a baking pan. Arrange the pan in the preheated zone 2. 7. Set the temperature to 200°C. Set the time to 14 to 18 minutes and select Roast or until tender for the zone 1. Set the time to 20 minutes and Bake or until a toothpick inserted in the centre of the bread comes out clean for the zone 2. Select START. 8. When the cooking is complete, remove the baking pan from the air fryer and allow the bread to cool for a few minutes before slicing to serve.

Peppery Brown Rice Fritters and Cheesy Potato Patties

Prep time: 15 minutes | Cook time: 10 minutes

Peppery Brown Rice Fritters| Serves 4:

- 1 (284 g) bag frozen cooked brown rice, thawed
- 1 egg
- 3 tablespoons brown rice flour
- 80 ml finely grated carrots
- 80 ml minced red pepper
- 2 tablespoons minced fresh basil
- 3 tablespoons grated Parmesan cheese
- 2 teaspoons olive oil

Cheesy Potato Patties | Serves 8
- 900 g white potatoes
- 120 ml finely chopped spring onions
- ½ teaspoon freshly ground black pepper, or more to taste
- 1 tablespoon fine sea salt
- ½ teaspoon hot paprika
- 475 ml shredded Colby or Monterey Jack cheese
- 60 ml rapeseed oil
- 235 ml crushed crackers

1. Preheat the air fryer to 180°C. In a small bowl, combine the thawed rice, egg, and flour and mix to blend. 2. Stir in the carrots, pepper, basil, and Parmesan cheese. 3. Form the mixture into 8 fritters and drizzle with the olive oil. 4. Boil the potatoes until soft. 5. Dry them off and peel them before mashing thoroughly, leaving no lumps. 6. Combine the mashed potatoes with spring onions, pepper, salt, paprika, and cheese. 7. Mould the mixture into balls with your hands and press with your palm to flatten them into patties. 8. In a shallow dish, combine the rapeseed oil and crushed crackers. 9. Put the fritters carefully into the zone 1. Coat the patties in the crumb mixture. Put the patties into the zone 2. 10. Set the temperature to 200°C. Set the time to 8 to 10 minutes, or until the fritters are golden brown and cooked through. Select AIR FRY for the zone 1 and Bake for the zone 2. Select START. 10. In multiple batches if necessary. Serve hot and immediately.

Rosemary and Orange Roasted Chickpeas

Prep time: 5 minutes | Cook time: 10 to 12 minutes | Makes 1 L

1 L cooked chickpeas	1 teaspoon paprika
2 tablespoons vegetable oil	Zest of 1 orange
1 teaspoon rock salt	1 tablespoon chopped fresh rosemary
1 teaspoon cumin	

1. Preheat the air fryer to 180°C. Make sure the chickpeas are completely dry prior to roasting. 2. In a medium bowl, toss the chickpeas with oil, salt, cumin, and paprika. 3. Working in batches, spread the chickpeas in a single layer in the dual zone. Set the temperature to 200°C. Set the time to 10 to 12 minutes until crisp, shaking once halfway through. Select AIR FRY. Select START. 4. Return the warm chickpeas to the bowl and toss with the orange zest and rosemary. 5. Allow to cool completely. Serve.

Air Fried Shishito Peppers and Easy Devils on Horseback

Prep time: 10 minutes | Cook time: 7 minutes Air Fried Shishito Peppers | Serves 4:

230 g shishito or Padron peppers (about 24)	Easy Devils on Horseback Serves 12:
1 tablespoon olive oil	24 small pitted prunes (128 g)
Coarse sea salt, to taste	60 ml crumbled blue cheese, divided
Lemon wedges, for serving	8 slices centre-cut bacon, cut crosswise into thirds
Cooking spray	

1. Preheat the air fryer to 180°C. 2. Spritz the zone 1 with cooking spray. Toss the peppers with olive oil in a large bowl to coat well. 3. Halve the prunes lengthwise, but don't cut them all the way through. 4. Place ½ teaspoon of cheese in the centre of each prune. 5. Wrap a piece of bacon around each prune and secure the bacon with a toothpick. 6. Arrange the peppers in the preheated zone 1. Working in batches, arrange a single layer of the prunes in the zone 2. 7. Set the temperature to 200°C. Set the time to 5 minutes or until blistered and lightly charred and about 7 minutes for the zone 2, flipping halfway, until the bacon is cooked through and crisp. Select AIR FRY. Select START. Shake the basket and sprinkle the peppers with salt halfway through the cooking time. Transfer the peppers onto a plate and squeeze the lemon wedges on top before serving. 8. Let cool slightly and serve warm.

Chapter 4 Poultry

Chapter 4 Poultry

Chicken Manchurian and Chicken Paillard

Prep time: 20 minutes | Cook time: 20 minutes | Serves 2

Chicken Manchurian:
450 g boneless, skinless chicken breasts, cut into 1-inch pieces
60 g ketchup
1 tablespoon tomato-based chili sauce, such as Heinz
1 tablespoon soy sauce
1 tablespoon rice vinegar
2 teaspoons vegetable oil
1 teaspoon hot sauce, such as Tabasco
½ teaspoon garlic powder
¼ teaspoon cayenne pepper
2 spring onions, thinly sliced
Cooked white rice, for serving
Chicken Paillard:
2 large eggs, room temperature
1 tablespoon water
40 g powdered Parmesan cheese or pork dust
2 teaspoons dried thyme leaves
1 teaspoon ground black pepper
2 (140 g) boneless, skinless chicken breasts, pounded to ½ inch thick
Lemon Butter Sauce:
2 tablespoons unsalted butter, melted
2 teaspoons lemon juice
¼ teaspoon finely chopped fresh thyme leaves, plus more for garnish
⅛ teaspoon fine sea salt
Lemon slices, for serving

1. Preheat the air fryer to 180°C. 2. In a bowl, combine the chicken, ketchup, chili sauce, soy sauce, vinegar, oil, hot sauce, garlic powder, cayenne, and three-quarters of the spring onions and toss until evenly coated. 3. Spray the zone 2 with avocado oil. 4. Beat the eggs in a shallow dish, then add the water and stir well. 5. In a separate shallow dish, mix together the Parmesan, thyme, and pepper until well combined. 6. One at a time, dip the chicken breasts in the eggs and let any excess drip off, then dredge both sides of the chicken in the Parmesan mixture. As you finish, set the coated chicken in the zone 2. 7. Scrape the chicken and sauce into a metal cake pan and place the pan in the zone 1. 8. Set the temperature to 200°C. Set the time to about 20 minutes and BAKE for the zone 1 until the chicken is cooked through and the sauce is reduced to a thick glaze. Set the time to 5 minutes and ROAST for the zone 2, flipping the chicken pieces halfway through. Select START. 9. Remove the pan from the air fryer. Spoon the chicken and sauce over rice and top with the remaining spring onions. Then flip the chicken and cook for another 5 minutes, or until cooked through and the internal temperature reaches 76°C. 10. While the chicken cooks, make the lemon butter sauce: In a small bowl, mix together all the sauce ingredients until well combined. 11. Plate the chicken and pour the sauce over it. Garnish with chopped fresh thyme and serve with lemon slices. 1. Store leftovers in an airtight container in the refrigerator for up to 4 days.

Chicken Schnitzel and Bacon-Wrapped Stuffed Chicken Breasts

Prep time: 30 minutes | Cook time: 30 minutes | Serves 4

Chicken Schnitzel:
60 g all-purpose flour
1 teaspoon marjoram
½ teaspoon thyme
1 teaspoon dried parsley flakes
½ teaspoon salt
1 egg
1 teaspoon lemon juice
1 teaspoon water
120 g breadcrumbs
4 chicken tenders, pounded thin, cut in half lengthwise
Cooking spray
Bacon-Wrapped Stuffed
Chicken Breasts:
80 g chopped frozen spinach, thawed and squeezed dry
55 g cream cheese, softened
20 g grated Parmesan cheese
1 jalapeño, seeded and chopped
½ teaspoon kosher salt
1 teaspoon black pepper
2 large boneless, skinless chicken breasts, butterflied and pounded to ½-inch thickness
4 teaspoons salt-free Cajun seasoning
6 slices bacon

1. Preheat the air fryer to 180°C and spritz with cooking spray. 2. Combine the flour, marjoram, thyme, parsley, and salt in a shallow dish. Stir to mix well. 3. Whisk the egg with lemon juice and water in a large bowl. Pour the breadcrumbs in a separate shallow dish. 4. Roll the chicken halves in the flour mixture first, then in the egg mixture, and then roll over the breadcrumbs to coat well. Shake the excess off. 5. In a small bowl, combine the spinach, cream cheese, Parmesan cheese, jalapeño, salt, and pepper. Stir until well combined. 6. Place the butterflied chicken breasts on a flat surface. Spread the cream cheese mixture evenly across each piece of chicken. Starting with the narrow end, roll up each chicken breast, ensuring the filling stays inside. Season chicken with the Cajun seasoning, patting it in to ensure it sticks to the meat. 7. Wrap each breast in 3 slices of bacon. Place in the zone 1. Arrange the chicken halves in the preheated zone 2 and spritz with cooking spray on both sides. 8. Set the temperature to 180°C for 30 minutes for the zone 1. Set the temperature to 5 minutes and 200°C for the zone 2, or until the chicken halves are golden brown and crispy. Select AIR FRY. Select START. 8. Use a meat thermometer to ensure the chicken has reached an internal temperature of 76°C. 9. Let the chicken stand 5 minutes before slicing each rolled-up breast in half to serve. Flip the halves halfway through. Serve immediately.

Peachy Chicken Chunks with Cherries and Thai Tacos with Peanut Sauce

Prep time: 18 minutes | Cook time: 14 minutes | Serves 4

100 g peach preserves
1 teaspoon ground rosemary
½ teaspoon black pepper
½ teaspoon salt
½ teaspoon marjoram
1 teaspoon light olive oil
450 g boneless chicken breasts, cut in 1½-inch chunks
Oil for misting or cooking spray
1 (280 g) package frozen unsweetened dark cherries, thawed and drained
Thai Tacos with Peanut Sauce:
450 g chicken mince
10 g diced onions (about 1 small onion)
2 cloves garlic, minced
¼ teaspoon fine sea salt
Sauce:
60 g creamy peanut butter, room temperature
2 tablespoons chicken broth, plus more if needed
2 tablespoons lime juice
2 tablespoons grated fresh ginger
2 tablespoons wheat-free tamari or coconut aminos
1½ teaspoons hot sauce
5 drops liquid stevia (optional)
For Serving:
2 small heads butter lettuce, leaves separated
Lime slices (optional)
For Garnish (Optional):
Coriander leaves
Shredded purple cabbage
Sliced green onions

1. Preheat the air fryer to 180°C. In a medium bowl, mix together peach preserves, rosemary, pepper, salt, marjoram, and olive oil. 2. Stir in chicken chunks and toss to coat well with the preserve mixture. 3. Spray the air fryer basket with oil or cooking spray and lay chicken chunks in the zone 1. 3. Make the sauce: In a medium-sized bowl, stir together the peanut butter, broth, lime juice, ginger, tamari, hot sauce, and stevia (if using) until well combined. If the sauce is too thick, add another tablespoon or two of broth. Taste and add more hot sauce if desired. 4. Add half of the sauce to the pan with the chicken. Cook for another minute, until heated through, and stir well to combine. 5. Assemble the tacos: Place several lettuce leaves on a serving plate. Place a few tablespoons of the chicken mixture in each lettuce leaf and garnish with coriander leaves, purple cabbage, and sliced green onions, if desired. Serve the remaining sauce on the side. 6. Serve with lime slices, if desired. Store leftover meat mixture in an airtight container in the refrigerator for up to 4 days; store leftover sauce, lettuce leaves, and garnishes separately. Reheat the meat mixture in a lightly greased pie pan in the zone 2. 7. Set the temperature to 200°C and the time to 7 minutes for the zone 1. Stir. Cook for 6 to 8 more minutes or until chicken juices run clear. Set the temperature to 180°C the time to 3 minutes for the zone 2, or until heated through. Select AIR FRY. Select START. 8. When chicken has cooked through, scatter the cherries over and cook for additional minute to heat cherries. 9. Place the chicken mince, onions, garlic, and salt in a pie pan or a dish that will fit in your air fryer. Break up the chicken with a spatula. Place in the zone 1 and bake for 5 minutes, or until the chicken is browned and cooked through. Break up the chicken again into small crumbles.

Chicken, Courgette, and Spinach Salad and South Indian Pepper Chicken

Prep time: 40 minutes | Cook time: 20 minutes | Serves 4

Chicken, Courgette, and Spinach Salad:
3 (140 g) boneless, skinless chicken breasts, cut into 1-inch cubes
5 teaspoons extra-virgin olive oil
½ teaspoon dried thyme
1 medium red onion, sliced
1 red bell pepper, sliced
1 small courgette, cut into strips
3 tablespoons freshly squeezed lemon juice
85 g fresh baby spinach leaves
South Indian Pepper Chicken:
Spice Mix:
1 dried red chili, or ½ teaspoon dried red pepper flakes
1-inch piece cinnamon or cassia bark
1½ teaspoons coriander seeds
1 teaspoon fennel seeds
1 teaspoon cumin seeds
1 teaspoon black peppercorns
½ teaspoon cardamom seeds
¼ teaspoon ground turmeric
1 teaspoon kosher salt
Chicken:
450 g boneless, skinless chicken thighs, cut crosswise into thirds
2 medium onions, cut into ½-inch-thick slices
60 ml olive oil
Cauliflower rice, steamed rice, or naan bread, for serving

1. Insert the crisper plate into the basket and the basket into the unit. 2. For the spice mix: Combine the dried chili, cinnamon, coriander, fennel, cumin, peppercorns, and cardamom in a clean coffee or spice grinder. Grind, shaking the grinder lightly so all the seeds and bits get into the blades, until the mixture is broken down to a fine powder. Stir in the turmeric and salt. 3. For the chicken: Place the chicken and onions in resealable plastic bag. Add the oil and 1½ tablespoons of the spice mix. Seal the bag and massage until the chicken is well coated. Marinate at room temperature for 30 minutes or in the refrigerator for up to 24 hours. 4. Place the chicken and onions in the zone 1. Once the unit is preheated, place the bowls into the zone 2. In two large bowls, combine the chicken, olive oil, and thyme. Toss to coat. Transfer to a medium metal bowl that fits into the basket. 5. Set the temperature to 190°C. Set the time to 3 minutes and ROAST for the zone 1. Set the time to 20 minutes and AIR FRY for the zone 2. Select START. 6. Then Add the red onion, red bell pepper, and courgette to the bowl. Resume cooking. After about 6 minutes more, stir the chicken and vegetables. Resume cooking. 7. When the cooking is complete, a food thermometer inserted into the chicken should register at least 76°C. Remove the bowl from the unit and stir in the lemon juice. 8. Put the spinach in a serving bowl and top with the chicken mixture. Toss to combine and serve immediately. 9. Use a meat thermometer to ensure the chicken has reached an internal temperature of 76°C. 10. Serve with steamed rice, cauliflower rice, or naan.

Chicken and Vegetable Fajitas

Prep time: 15 minutes | Cook time: 23 minutes | Serves 6

Chicken:
450 g boneless, skinless chicken thighs, cut crosswise into thirds
1 tablespoon vegetable oil
4½ teaspoons taco seasoning
Vegetables:
50 g sliced onion
150 g sliced bell pepper
1 or 2 jalapeños, quartered lengthwise
1 tablespoon vegetable oil
½ teaspoon kosher salt
½ teaspoon ground cumin
For Serving:
Tortillas
Sour cream
Shredded cheese
Guacamole
Salsa

1. For the chicken: In a medium bowl, toss together the chicken, vegetable oil, and taco seasoning to coat. 2. For the vegetables: In a separate bowl, toss together the onion, bell pepper, jalapeño(s), vegetable oil, salt, and cumin to coat. 3. Place the chicken in the dual zone. Set the air fryer to (190ºC for 10 minutes. Select START. Add the vegetables to the basket, toss everything together to blend the seasonings, and set the air fryer for 13 minutes more. Use a meat thermometer to ensure the chicken has reached an internal temperature of 76ºC. 4. Transfer the chicken and vegetables to a serving platter. Serve with tortillas and the desired fajita fixings.

Coriander Lime Chicken Thighs and Celery Chicken

Prep time: 25 minutes | Cook time: 22 minutes | Serves 4

Coriander Lime Chicken Thighs:
4 bone-in, skin-on chicken thighs
1 teaspoon baking powder
½ teaspoon garlic powder
2 teaspoons chili powder
1 teaspoon cumin
2 medium limes
5 g chopped fresh coriander
Celery Chicken:
120 ml soy sauce
2 tablespoons hoisin sauce
4 teaspoons minced garlic
1 teaspoon freshly ground black pepper
8 boneless, skinless chicken tenderloins
120 g chopped celery
1 medium red bell pepper, diced
Olive oil spray

1. Preheat the air fryer to 190ºC. Pat chicken thighs dry and sprinkle with baking powder. 2. In a small bowl, mix garlic powder, chili powder, and cumin and sprinkle evenly over thighs, gently rubbing on and under chicken skin.3. Spray the zone 2 lightly with olive oil spray. 4. In a large bowl, mix together the soy sauce, hoisin sauce, garlic, and black pepper to make a marinade. Add the chicken, celery, and bell pepper and toss to coat. 5. Cut one lime in half and squeeze juice over thighs. Place chicken into the zone 1. 5. Shake the excess marinade off the chicken, place it and the vegetables in the zone 2, and lightly spray with olive oil spray. You may need to cook them in batches. Reserve the remaining marinade. 4. Set the temperature to 190ºC. Set the time to 22 minutes and ROAST for the zone 1. Set the time to 8 minutes and AIR FRY. Select START. Turn the chicken over and brush with some of the remaining marinade. 6. Cut other lime into four wedges for serving and garnish cooked chicken with wedges and coriander. 7. Air fry for an additional 5 to 7 minutes, or until the chicken reaches an internal temperature of at least 76ºC. Serve.

Potato-Crusted Chicken and Simply Terrific Turkey Meatballs

Prep time: 25 minutes | Cook time: 22 minutes | Serves 4

Potato-Crusted Chicken:
60 g buttermilk
1 large egg, beaten
180 g instant potato flakes
20 g grated Parmesan cheese
1 teaspoon salt
½ teaspoon freshly ground black pepper
2 whole boneless, skinless chicken breasts (about 450 g each), halved
1 to 2 tablespoons oil
Simply Terrific Turkey
Meatballs:
1 red bell pepper, seeded and coarsely chopped
2 cloves garlic, coarsely chopped
15 g chopped fresh parsley
680 g 85% lean turkey mince
1 egg, lightly beaten
45 g grated Parmesan cheese
1 teaspoon salt
½ teaspoon freshly ground black pepper

1. Preheat the air fryer to 180ºC. In a shallow bowl, whisk the buttermilk and egg until blended. In another shallow bowl, stir together the potato flakes, cheese, salt, and pepper. 2. One at a time, dip the chicken pieces in the buttermilk mixture and the potato flake mixture, coating thoroughly. 3. In a food processor fitted with a metal blade, combine the bell pepper, garlic, and parsley. Pulse until finely chopped. Transfer the vegetables to a large mixing bowl. 4. Add the turkey, egg, Parmesan, salt, and black pepper. Mix gently until thoroughly combined. Shape the mixture into 1¼-inch meatballs. 4. Line the air fryer basket with parchment paper. 5. Place the coated chicken on the parchment in the zone 1 and spritz with oil. Working in batches if necessary, arrange the meatballs in a single layer in the zone 2. 6. Set the temperature to 200ºC. Set the time to 15 minutes for the zone 1 and 7 to 10 minutes for the zone 2. Select AIR FRY. Select START. Flip the chicken, spritz it with oil, and cook for 7 to 10 minutes more until the outside is crispy and the inside is no longer pink. 7. Coat lightly with olive oil spray. Pausing halfway through the cooking time to shake the basket, until lightly browned and a thermometer inserted into the centre of a meatball registers 76ºC.

Piri-Piri Chicken Thighs

Prep time: 5 minutes | Cook time: 25 minutes | Serves 4

60 ml piri-piri sauce	1 tablespoon extra-virgin olive oil
1 tablespoon freshly squeezed lemon juice	4 bone-in, skin-on chicken thighs, each weighing approximately 200 to 230 g
2 tablespoons brown sugar, divided	½ teaspoon cornflour
2 cloves garlic, minced	

1. To make the marinade, whisk together the piri-piri sauce, lemon juice, 1 tablespoon of brown sugar, and the garlic in a small bowl. While whisking, slowly pour in the oil in a steady stream and continue to whisk until emulsified. Using a skewer, poke holes in the chicken thighs and place them in a small glass dish. Pour the marinade over the chicken and turn the thighs to coat them with the sauce. Cover the dish and refrigerate for at least 15 minutes and up to 1 hour. 2. Preheat the air fryer to 190°C. Remove the chicken thighs from the dish, reserving the marinade, and place them skin-side down in the dual zone air fryer. Select MATCH COOK. Select START. Air fry until the internal temperature reaches 76°C, 15 to 20 minutes. 3. Meanwhile, whisk the remaining brown sugar and the cornflour into the marinade and microwave it on high power for 1 minute until it is bubbling and thickened to a glaze. 4. Once the chicken is cooked, turn the thighs over and brush them with the glaze. Air fry for a few additional minutes until the glaze browns and begins to char in spots. 5. Remove the chicken to a platter and serve with additional piri-piri sauce, if desired.

Crunchy Chicken Tenders and Lemon-Basil Turkey Breasts

Prep time: 35 minutes | Cook time: 58 minutes | Serves 4

Crunchy Chicken Tenders:	1 lemon, quartered
1 egg	Lemon-Basil Turkey Breasts:
60 ml unsweetened almond milk	2 tablespoons olive oil
30 g whole wheat flour	900 g turkey breasts, bone-in, skin-on
30 g whole wheat bread crumbs	Coarse sea salt and ground black pepper, to taste
½ teaspoon salt	1 teaspoon fresh basil leaves, chopped
½ teaspoon black pepper	2 tablespoons lemon zest, grated
½ teaspoon dried thyme	
½ teaspoon dried sage	
½ teaspoon garlic powder	
450 g chicken tenderloins	

1. Preheat the air fryer to 180°C. 2. In a shallow bowl, beat together the egg and almond milk until frothy. 3. In a separate shallow bowl, whisk together the flour, bread crumbs, salt, pepper, thyme, sage, and garlic powder. 4. Dip each chicken tenderloin into the egg mixture, then into the bread crumb mixture, coating the outside with the crumbs. Place the breaded chicken tenderloins into the bottom of the zone 1 in an even layer, making sure that they don't touch each other. 5. Rub olive oil on all sides of the turkey breasts; sprinkle with salt, pepper, basil, and lemon zest. 6. Place the turkey breasts skin side up on the parchment-lined zone 2. 7. Set the trmperature 200°C for 6 minutes for the zone 1. Set the temperature to 170°C for 30 minutes for the zone 2. Select AIR FRY. Select START, then turn and cook for an additional 5 to 6 minutes. Serve with lemon slices. Now, turn them over and cook an additional 28 minutes. 8. Serve with lemon wedges, if desired. Bon appétit!

Herb-Buttermilk Chicken Breast and Nice Goulash

Prep time: 5 minutes | Cook time: 40 minutes | Serves 2

Herb-Buttermilk Chicken Breast:	Cooking spray
1 large bone-in, skin-on chicken breast	Prep time: 5 minutes	Cook time: 17 minutes	Serves 2
240 ml buttermilk	Nice Goulash:
1½ teaspoons dried parsley	2 red bell peppers, chopped
1½ teaspoons dried chives	450 g chicken mince
¾ teaspoon kosher salt	2 medium tomatoes, diced
½ teaspoon dried dill	120 ml chicken broth
½ teaspoon onion powder	Salt and ground black pepper, to taste
¼ teaspoon garlic powder	Cooking spray
¼ teaspoon dried tarragon	

1. Preheat the air fryer to 180°C. Place the chicken breast in a bowl and pour over the buttermilk, turning the chicken in it to make sure it's completely covered. Let the chicken stand at room temperature for at least 20 minutes or in the refrigerator for up to 4 hours. 2. Meanwhile, in a bowl, stir together the parsley, chives, salt, dill, onion powder, garlic powder, and tarragon. 3. Remove the chicken from the buttermilk, letting the excess drip off, then place the chicken skin-side up directly in the zone 1. Sprinkle the seasoning mix all over the top of the chicken breast, then let stand until the herb mix soaks into the buttermilk, at least 5 minutes. 5. Spray the top of the chicken with cooking spray. 4. Spritz a baking pan with cooking spray. 6. Set the bell pepper in the baking pan and put in the zone 2. Add the chicken mince and diced tomatoes in the zone 2 and stir to mix well. 7. Set the temperature to 200°C for 5 minutes or until the bell pepper is tender in the zone 1. Set the temperature to 180°C and the time to 30 to 35 minutes. Select AIR FRY for the zone 1 and BAKE for the zone 8. Select START. Shake the basket halfway through. Bake until an instant-read thermometer inserted into the thickest part of the breast reads 80°C and the chicken is deep golden brown. 9. Transfer the chicken breast to a cutting board, let rest for 10 minutes, then cut the meat off the bone and cut into thick slices for serving. Broil for 6 more minutes or until the chicken is lightly browned. 10. Pour the chicken broth over and sprinkle with salt and ground black pepper. Stir to mix well. Broil for an additional 6 minutes. Serve immediately.

Herbed Roast Chicken Breast

Prep time: 10 minutes | Cook time: 25 minutes | Serves 2 to 4

2 tablespoons salted butter or ghee, at room temperature	½ teaspoon smoked paprika
1 teaspoon dried Italian seasoning, crushed	¼ teaspoon black pepper
	2 bone-in, skin-on chicken breast halves (280 g each)
½ teaspoon kosher salt	Lemon wedges, for serving

1. In a small bowl, stir together the butter, Italian seasoning, salt, paprika, and pepper until thoroughly combined. 2. Using a small sharp knife, carefully loosen the skin on each chicken breast half, starting at the thin end of each. Very carefully separate the skin from the flesh, leaving the skin attached at the thick end of each breast. Divide the herb butter into quarters. Rub one-quarter of the butter onto the flesh of each breast. Fold and lightly press the skin back onto each breast. Rub the remaining butter onto the skin of each breast. 3. Place the chicken in the dual zone air fryer. Set the air fryer to (190ºC for 25 minutes. Select START. Use a meat thermometer to ensure the chicken breasts have reached an internal temperature of 76ºC. 4. Transfer the chicken to a cutting board. Lightly cover with aluminum foil and let rest for 5 to 10 minutes. 5. Serve with lemon wedges.

Personal Cauliflower Pizzas

Prep time: 10 minutes | Cook time: 25 minutes | Serves 2

1 (340 g) bag frozen riced cauliflower	4 tablespoons no-sugar-added marinara sauce, divided
75 g shredded Mozzarella cheese	110 g fresh Mozzarella, chopped, divided
25 g almond flour	140 g cooked chicken breast, chopped, divided
20 g Parmesan cheese	
1 large egg	100 g chopped cherry tomatoes, divided
½ teaspoon salt	
1 teaspoon garlic powder	5 g fresh baby rocket, divided
1 teaspoon dried oregano	

1. Preheat the air fryer to 200ºC. Cut 4 sheets of parchment paper to fit the basket of the air fryer. Brush with olive oil and set aside. 2. In a large glass bowl, microwave the cauliflower according to package directions. Place the cauliflower on a clean towel, draw up the sides, and squeeze tightly over a sink to remove the excess moisture. Return the cauliflower to the bowl and add the shredded Mozzarella along with the almond flour, Parmesan, egg, salt, garlic powder, and oregano. Stir until thoroughly combined. 3. Divide the dough into two equal portions. Place one piece of dough on the prepared parchment paper and pat gently into a thin, flat disk 7 to 8 inches in diameter. Air fry for 15 minutes until the crust begins to brown. Let cool for 5 minutes. 4. Transfer the parchment paper with the crust on top to a baking sheet. Place a second sheet of parchment paper over the crust. While holding the edges of both sheets together, carefully lift the crust off the baking sheet, flip it, and place it back in the air fryer basket. The new sheet of parchment paper is now on the bottom. Remove the top piece of paper and air fry the crust for another 15 minutes until the top begins to brown. Remove the basket from the air fryer. 5. Spread 2 tablespoons of the marinara sauce on top of the crust, followed by half the fresh Mozzarella, chicken, cherry tomatoes, and rocket. Air fry for 5 to 10 minutes longer, until the cheese is melted and beginning to brown. Remove the pizza from the oven and let it sit for 10 minutes before serving. Repeat with the remaining ingredients to make a second pizza. Dual zone air fryer can be used to make two pieces at the same time.

Chicken Thighs with Coriander and Bell Pepper Stuffed Chicken Roll-Ups

Prep time: 25 minutes | Cook time: 25 minutes | Serves 4

Chicken Thighs with Coriander:	Roll-Ups:
1 tablespoon olive oil	2 (115 g) boneless, skinless chicken breasts, slice in half horizontally
Juice of ½ lime	
1 tablespoon coconut aminos	
1½ teaspoons Montreal chicken seasoning	1 tablespoon olive oil
	Juice of ½ lime
8 bone-in chicken thighs, skin on	2 tablespoons taco seasoning
	½ green bell pepper, cut into strips
2 tablespoons chopped fresh coriander	½ red bell pepper, cut into strips
Bell Pepper Stuffed Chicken	¼ onion, sliced

1.Preheat the air fryer to 180ºC. In a gallon-size resealable bag, combine the olive oil, lime juice, coconut aminos, and chicken seasoning. Add the chicken thighs, seal the bag, and massage the bag to ensure the chicken is thoroughly coated. Refrigerate for at least 2 hours, preferably overnight. 2. Remove the chicken from the marinade (discard the marinade) and arrange in a single layer in the zone 1. Pausing halfway through the cooking time to flip the chicken. 3. Unfold the chicken breast slices on a clean work surface. Rub with olive oil, then drizzle with lime juice and sprinkle with taco seasoning. 4. Top the chicken slices with equal amount of bell peppers and onion. Roll them up and secure with toothpicks. 5. Arrange the chicken roll-ups in the preheated zone 2. 6. Set the temperature to 200ºC. Set the time to 20 to 25 minutes for the zone 1 and 12 minutes for the zone 2 until a thermometer inserted into the thickest part registers 76ºC and the internal temperature of the chicken reaches at least 76ºC. Flip the chicken roll-ups halfway through. 7. Transfer the chicken to a serving platter and top with the coriander before serving. 8. Remove the chicken from the air fryer. Discard the toothpicks and serve immediately.

Stuffed Turkey Roulade

Prep time: 10 minutes | Cook time: 45 minutes | Serves 4

1 (900 g) boneless turkey breast, skin removed
1 teaspoon salt
½ teaspoon black pepper
115 g goat cheese
1 tablespoon fresh thyme
1 tablespoon fresh sage
2 garlic cloves, minced
2 tablespoons olive oil
Fresh chopped parsley, for garnish

1. Preheat the air fryer to 180ºC. 2. Using a sharp knife, butterfly the turkey breast, and season both sides with salt and pepper and set aside. 3. In a small bowl, mix together the goat cheese, thyme, sage, and garlic. 4. Spread the cheese mixture over the turkey breast, then roll it up tightly, tucking the ends underneath. 5. Place the turkey breast roulade onto a piece of aluminum foil, wrap it up, and place it into the dual zone air fryer. 6. Bake for 30 minutes. Select START. Remove the foil from the turkey breast and brush the top with oil, then continue cooking for another 10 to 15 minutes, or until the outside has browned and the internal temperature reaches 76ºC. 7. Remove and cut into 1-inch-wide slices and serve with a sprinkle of parsley on top.

Spice-Rubbed Turkey Breast and Sweet Chili Spiced Chicken

Prep time: 15 minutes | Cook time: 50 minutes | Serves 10

Spice-Rubbed Turkey Breast:
1 tablespoon sea salt
1 teaspoon paprika
1 teaspoon onion powder
1 teaspoon garlic powder
½ teaspoon freshly ground black pepper
1.8 kg bone-in, skin-on turkey breast
2 tablespoons unsalted butter, melted
Sweet Chili Spice Rub | Serves 4:
2 tablespoons brown sugar
2 tablespoons paprika
1 teaspoon dry mustard powder
1 teaspoon chili powder
2 tablespoons coarse sea salt or kosher salt
2 teaspoons coarsely ground black pepper
1 tablespoon vegetable oil
1 (1.6 kg) chicken, cut into 8 pieces

1. Set the air fryer to 180ºC. 2. In a small bowl, combine the salt, paprika, onion powder, garlic powder, and pepper. 3. Prepare the spice rub by combining the brown sugar, paprika, mustard powder, chili powder, salt and pepper. Rub the oil all over the chicken pieces and then rub the spice mix onto the chicken, covering completely. This is done very easily in a zipper sealable bag. You can do this ahead of time and let the chicken marinate in the refrigerator, or just proceed with cooking right away. 4. Sprinkle the seasonings all over the turkey. Brush the turkey with some of the melted butter. Place the turkey in the zone 1, skin-side down. Air fry the chicken in two batches. Place the two chicken thighs and two drumsticks into the zone 2. 5. Set the temperature 200ºC for 25 minutes for the zone 1. Set the temperature to 190ºC for 10 minutes. Select ROAST for the zone 1 and AIR FRY for the zone 2. Select START. Then, gently turn the chicken pieces over and air fry for another 10 minutes. Flip the turkey and brush it with the remaining butter. Continue cooking for another 20 to 30 minutes, until an instant-read thermometer reads 70ºC. 6. Remove the turkey breast from the air fryer. Tent a piece of aluminum foil over the turkey, and allow it to rest for about 5 minutes before serving. 7. Remove the chicken pieces and let them rest on a plate while you cook the chicken breasts. Air fry the chicken breasts, skin side down for 8 minutes. 8. Turn the chicken breasts over and air fry for another 12 minutes. 9. Lower the temperature of the air fryer to 170ºC. Place the first batch of chicken on top of the second batch already in the basket and air fry for a final 3 minutes. 10. Let the chicken rest for 5 minutes and serve warm with some mashed potatoes and a green salad or vegetables.

African Piri-Piri Chicken Drumsticks

Prep time: 30 minutes | Cook time: 20 minutes | Serves 2

Chicken:
1 tablespoon chopped fresh thyme leaves
1 tablespoon minced fresh ginger
1 small shallot, finely chopped
2 garlic cloves, minced
80 ml piri-piri sauce or hot sauce
3 tablespoons extra-virgin olive oil
Zest and juice of 1 lemon
1 teaspoon smoked paprika
½ teaspoon kosher salt
½ teaspoon black pepper
4 chicken drumsticks
Glaze:
2 tablespoons butter or ghee
1 teaspoon chopped fresh thyme leaves
1 garlic clove, minced
1 tablespoon piri-piri sauce
1 tablespoon fresh lemon juice

1. For the chicken: In a small bowl, stir together all the ingredients except the chicken. Place the chicken and the marinade in a gallon-size resealable plastic bag. Seal the bag and massage to coat. Refrigerate for at least 2 hours or up to 24 hours, turning the bag occasionally. 2. Place the chicken legs in the dual zone air fryer. Set the air fryer to 200ºC for 20 minutes. Select START, turning the chicken halfway through the cooking time. 3. Meanwhile, for the glaze: Melt the butter in a small saucepan over medium-high heat. Add the thyme and garlic. Cook, stirring, until the garlic just begins to brown, 1 to 2 minutes. Add the piri-piri sauce and lemon juice. Reduce the heat to medium-low and simmer for 1 to 2 minutes. 4. Transfer the chicken to a serving platter. Pour the glaze over the chicken. Serve immediately.

Chicken Breasts with Asparagus, Beans, and Rocket

Prep time: 20 minutes | Cook time: 25 minutes | Serves 2

160 g canned cannellini beans, rinsed
1½ tablespoons red wine vinegar
1 garlic clove, minced
2 tablespoons extra-virgin olive oil, divided
Salt and ground black pepper, to taste
½ red onion, sliced thinly
230 g asparagus, trimmed and cut into 1-inch lengths
2 (230 g) boneless, skinless chicken breasts, trimmed
¼ teaspoon paprika
½ teaspoon ground coriander
60 g baby rocket, rinsed and drained

1. Preheat the air fryer to 200°C. 2. Warm the beans in microwave for 1 minutes and combine with red wine vinegar, garlic, 1 tablespoon of olive oil, ¼ teaspoon of salt, and ¼ teaspoon of ground black pepper in a bowl. Stir to mix well. 3. Combine the onion with ⅛ teaspoon of salt, ⅛ teaspoon of ground black pepper, and 2 teaspoons of olive oil in a separate bowl. Toss to coat well. 4. Place the onion in the zone 1 and air fry for 2 minutes, then add the asparagus and air fry for 8 more minutes or until the asparagus is tender. Shake the basket halfway through. Transfer the onion and asparagus to the bowl with beans. Set aside. 5. Toss the chicken breasts with remaining ingredients, except for the baby rocket, in a large bowl. 6. Put the chicken breasts in the zone 2 and air fry for 14 minutes or until the internal temperature of the chicken reaches at least 76°C. Flip the breasts halfway through. 7. Remove the chicken from the air fryer and serve on an aluminum foil with asparagus, beans, onion, and rocket. Sprinkle with salt and ground black pepper. Toss to serve.

Korean Honey Wings

Prep time: 10 minutes | Cook time: 25 minutes per batch | Serves 4

55 g gochujang, or red pepper paste
55 g mayonnaise
2 tablespoons honey
1 tablespoon sesame oil
2 teaspoons minced garlic
1 tablespoon sugar
2 teaspoons ground ginger
1.4 kg whole chicken wings
Olive oil spray
1 teaspoon salt
½ teaspoon freshly ground black pepper

1. In a large bowl, whisk the gochujang, mayonnaise, honey, sesame oil, garlic, sugar, and ginger. Set aside. 2. Insert the crisper plate into the basket and the basket into the unit. Preheat the unit by selecting AIR FRY, setting the temperature to 200°C, and setting the time to 3 minutes. Select START to begin. 3. To prepare the chicken wings, cut the wings in half. The meatier part is the drumette. Cut off and discard the wing tip from the flat part (or save the wing tips in the freezer to make chicken stock). 4. Once the unit is preheated, spray the crisper plate with olive oil. Working in batches, place the chicken wings into the dual zone, spray them with olive oil, and sprinkle with the salt and pepper. 5. Select AIR FRY, set the temperature to 200°C, and set the time to 20 minutes. Select START to begin. 6. After 10 minutes, remove the basket, flip the wings, and spray them with more olive oil. Reinsert the basket to resume cooking. 7. Cook the wings to an internal temperature of 76°C, then transfer them to the bowl with the prepared sauce and toss to coat. 8. Repeat steps 4, 5, 6, and 7 for the remaining chicken wings. 9. Return the coated wings to the dual zone and air fry for 4 to 6 minutes more until the sauce has glazed the wings and the chicken is crisp. After 3 minutes, check the wings to make sure they aren't burning. Serve hot.

Hoisin Turkey Burgers and Chicken with Pineapple and Peach

Prep time: 40 minutes | Cook time: 20 minutes | Serves 4

Hoisin Turkey Burgers:
Olive oil
450 g lean turkey mince
30 g whole-wheat bread crumbs
60 ml hoisin sauce
2 tablespoons soy sauce
4 whole-wheat buns
Chicken with Pineapple and Peach:
1 (450 g) low-sodium boneless, skinless chicken breasts, cut into 1-inch pieces
1 medium red onion, chopped
1 (230 g) can pineapple chunks, drained, 60 ml juice reserved
1 tablespoon peanut oil or safflower oil
1 peach, peeled, pitted, and cubed
1 tablespoon cornflour
½ teaspoon ground ginger
¼ teaspoon ground allspice
Brown rice, cooked (optional)

1. Preheat the air fryer to 180°C. Spray the air fryer basket lightly with olive oil. 2. In a large bowl, mix together the turkey, bread crumbs, hoisin sauce, and soy sauce. 3. Form the mixture into 4 equal patties. Cover with plastic wrap and refrigerate the patties for 30 minutes. 4. Place the patties in the zone 1 in a single layer. Spray the patties lightly with olive oil. 5. In a medium metal bowl, mix the chicken, red onion, pineapple, and peanut oil. Bake in the zone 2 for 9 minutes. Remove and stir. 6. Add the peach and return the bowl to the zone 2. 7. Set the temperature to 190°C and AIR FRY for 10 minutes for the zone 1. Set the temperature to 190°C and Bake for 3 minutes more for the zone 2. Select START. Remove and stir again. Flip the patties over, lightly spray with olive oil, and cook until golden brown, an additional 5 to 10 minutes. 8. Place the patties on buns and top with your choice of low-calorie burger toppings like sliced tomatoes, onions, and cabbage slaw. 9. In a small bowl, whisk the reserved pineapple juice, the cornflour, ginger, and allspice well. Add to the chicken mixture and stir to combine. 10. Bake for 2 to 3 minutes more, or until the chicken reaches an internal temperature of 76°C on a meat thermometer and the sauce is slightly thickened. 11. Serve immediately over hot cooked brown rice, if desired.

Chapter 5 Beef, Pork, and Lamb

Chapter 5 Beef, Pork, and Lamb

Spaghetti Zoodles and Meatballs

Prep time: 30 minutes | Cook time: 11 to 13 minutes | Serves 6

450 g beef mince	Freshly ground black pepper, to taste
1½ teaspoons sea salt, plus more for seasoning	Avocado oil spray
1 large egg, beaten	Keto-friendly marinara sauce, for serving
1 teaspoon gelatin	
180 ml Parmesan cheese	170 g courgette noodles, made using a spiralizer or store-bought
2 teaspoons minced garlic	
1 teaspoon Italian seasoning	

1. Place the beef mince in a large bowl, and season with the salt. 2. Place the egg in a separate bowl and sprinkle with the gelatin. Allow to sit for 5 minutes. 3. Stir the gelatin mixture, then pour it over the ground beef. Add the Parmesan, garlic, and Italian seasoning. Season with salt and pepper. 4. Form the mixture into 1½-inch meatballs and place them on a plate; cover with plastic wrap and refrigerate for at least 1 hour or overnight. 5. Spray the meatballs with oil. Set the air fryer to 200°C and arrange the meatballs in a single layer in the zone 1 air fryer. Air fry for 4 minutes. Flip the meatballs and spray them with more oil. Air fry for 4 minutes more, until an instant-read thermometer reads 72°C. Transfer the meatballs to a plate and allow them to rest. 6. While the meatballs are resting, heat the marinara in a saucepan on the stove over medium heat. 7. Place the courgette noodles in the zone 2 air fryer, and cook at 200°C for 3 to 5 minutes. 8. To serve, place the courgette noodles in serving bowls. Top with meatballs and warm marinara.

Panko Pork Chops

Prep time: 10 minutes | Cook time: 12 minutes | Serves 4

4 boneless pork chops, excess fat trimmed	1½ teaspoons paprika
¼ teaspoon salt	½ teaspoon granulated garlic
2 eggs	½ teaspoon onion granules
355 ml panko bread crumbs	1 teaspoon chili powder
3 tablespoons grated Parmesan cheese	¼ teaspoon freshly ground black pepper
	Olive oil spray

1. Sprinkle the pork chops with salt on both sides and let them sit while you prepare the seasonings and egg wash. 2. In a shallow medium bowl, beat the eggs. 3. In another shallow medium bowl, stir together the panko, Parmesan cheese, paprika, granulated garlic, onion granules, chili powder, and pepper. 4. Dip the pork chops in the egg and in the panko mixture to coat. Firmly press the crumbs onto the chops. 5. Insert the crisper plate into the dual zone and the basket into the unit. Preheat the unit by selecting AIR ROAST, setting the temperature to 200°C, and setting the time to 3 minutes. Select START to begin. 6. Once the unit is preheated, spray the crisper plate with olive oil. Place the pork chops into the dual zone and spray them with olive oil. 7. Select AIR ROAST, set the temperature to 200°C, and set the time to 12 minutes. Select START to begin. 8. After 6 minutes, flip the pork chops and spray them with more olive oil. Resume cooking. 9. When the cooking is complete, the chops should be golden and crispy and a food thermometer should register 64°C. Serve immediately.

Broccoli and Pork Teriyaki

Prep time: 10 minutes | Cook time: 13 minutes | Serves 4

1 head broccoli, trimmed into florets	450 g pork tenderloin, trimmed and cut into 1-inch pieces
1 tablespoon extra-virgin olive oil	120 ml teriyaki sauce, divided
	Olive oil spray
¼ teaspoon sea salt	475 ml cooked brown rice
¼ teaspoon freshly ground black pepper	Sesame seeds, for garnish

1. Insert the crisper plate into the basket and the basket into the unit. Preheat the unit by selecting AIR ROAST, setting the temperature to 200°C, and setting the time to 3 minutes. Select START to begin. 2. In a large bowl, toss together the broccoli, olive oil, salt, and pepper. 3. In a medium bowl, toss together the pork and 3 tablespoons of teriyaki sauce to coat the meat. 4. Once the unit is preheated, spray the crisper plate with olive oil. Put the broccoli and pork into the dual zone air fryer. Spray them with olive oil and drizzle with 1 tablespoon of teriyaki sauce. 5. Select AIR ROAST, set the temperature to 200°C, and set the time to 13 minutes. Select START to begin. 6. After 10 to 12 minutes, the broccoli is tender and light golden brown and a food thermometer inserted into the pork should register 64°C. Remove the basket and drizzle the broccoli and pork with the remaining 60 ml of teriyaki sauce and toss to coat. Reinsert the basket to resume cooking for 1 minute. 7. When the cooking is complete, serve immediately over the hot cooked rice, if desired, garnished with the sesame seeds.

Kheema Burgers

Prep time: 15 minutes | Cook time: 12 minutes | Serves 4

Burgers:
450 g 85% lean beef mince or lamb mince
2 large eggs, lightly beaten
1 medium brown onion, diced
60 ml chopped fresh coriander
1 tablespoon minced fresh ginger
3 cloves garlic, minced
2 teaspoons garam masala
1 teaspoon ground turmeric
½ teaspoon ground cinnamon
⅛ teaspoon ground cardamom
1 teaspoon coarse or flaky salt
1 teaspoon cayenne pepper
Raita Sauce:
235 ml grated cucumber
120 ml sour cream
¼ teaspoon coarse or flaky salt
¼ teaspoon black pepper
For Serving:
4 lettuce leaves, hamburger buns, or naan breads

1. For the burgers: In a large bowl, combine the beef mince, eggs, onion, coriander, ginger, garlic, garam masala, turmeric, cinnamon, cardamom, salt, and cayenne. Gently mix until ingredients are thoroughly combined. 2. Divide the meat into four portions and form into round patties. Make a slight depression in the middle of each patty with your thumb to prevent them from puffing up into a dome shape while cooking. 3. Place the patties in the dyal zone air fryer. Set the air fryer to 180°C for 12 minutes. Use a meat thermometer to ensure the burgers have reached an internal temperature of 72°C (for medium). 4. Meanwhile, for the sauce: In a small bowl, combine the cucumber, sour cream, salt, and pepper. 5. To serve: Place the burgers on the lettuce, buns, or naan and top with the sauce.

Mushroom in Bacon-Wrapped Filets Mignons

Prep time: 10 minutes | Cook time: 13 minutes per batch | Serves 8

30 g dried porcini mushrooms
½ teaspoon granulated white sugar
½ teaspoon salt
½ teaspoon ground white pepper
8 (110 g) filets mignons or beef fillet steaks
8 thin-cut bacon strips

1. Preheat the air fryer to 180°C. 2. Put the mushrooms, sugar, salt, and white pepper in a spice grinder and grind to combine. 3. On a clean work surface, rub the filets mignons with the mushroom mixture, then wrap each filet with a bacon strip. Secure with toothpicks if necessary. 4. Arrange the bacon-wrapped filets mignons in the preheated dual zone air fryer, seam side down. Work in batches to avoid overcrowding. 5. Air fry for 13 minutes or until medium rare. Select START to begin. Flip the filets halfway through. 6. Serve immediately.

Greek Lamb Pitta Pockets

Prep time: 15 minutes | Cook time: 6 minutes | Serves 4

Dressing:
235 ml plain yogurt
1 tablespoon lemon juice
1 teaspoon dried dill, crushed
1 teaspoon ground oregano
½ teaspoon salt
Meatballs:
230 g lamb mince
1 tablespoon diced onion
1 teaspoon dried parsley
1 teaspoon dried dill, crushed
¼ teaspoon oregano
¼ teaspoon coriander
¼ teaspoon ground cumin
¼ teaspoon salt
4 pitta halves
Suggested Toppings:
1 red onion, slivered
1 medium cucumber, deseeded, thinly sliced
Crumbled feta cheese
Sliced black olives
Chopped fresh peppers

1. Preheat the air fryer to 180°C. 2. Stir the dressing ingredients together in a small bowl and refrigerate while preparing lamb. 3. Combine all meatball ingredients in a large bowl and stir to distribute seasonings. 4. Shape meat mixture into 12 small meatballs, rounded or slightly flattened if you prefer. 5. Transfer the meatballs in the preheated dual zone and air fry for 6 minutes, until well done. Remove and drain on paper towels. 6. To serve, pile meatballs and the choice of toppings in pitta pockets and drizzle with dressing.

Tomato and Bacon Zoodles

Prep time: 10 minutes | Cook time: 15 to 22 minutes | Serves 2

230 g sliced bacon
120 ml baby plum tomatoes
1 large courgette, spiralized
120 ml ricotta cheese
60 ml double/whipping cream
80 ml finely grated Parmesan cheese, plus more for serving
Sea salt and freshly ground black pepper, to taste

1. Set the air fryer to 180°C. Arrange the bacon strips in a single layer in the dual zone air fryer—some overlapping is okay because the bacon will shrink, but cook in batches if needed. Air fry for 8 minutes. Flip the bacon strips and air fry for 2 to 5 minutes more, until the bacon is crisp. Remove the bacon from the air fryer. 2. Put the tomatoes in the zone 1 and air fry for 3 to 5 minutes, until they are just starting to burst. Remove the tomatoes from the air fryer. 3. Put the courgette noodles in the zone 2 air fryer and air fry for 2 to 4 minutes, to the desired doneness. 4. Meanwhile, combine the ricotta, cream, and Parmesan in a saucepan over medium-low heat. Cook, stirring often, until warm and combined. 5. Crumble the bacon. Place the courgette, bacon, and tomatoes in a bowl. Toss with the ricotta sauce. Season with salt and pepper, and sprinkle with additional Parmesan.

Chinese-Style Baby Back Ribs

Prep time: 30 minutes | Cook time: 30 minutes | Serves 4

1 tablespoon toasted sesame oil	1 tablespoon agave nectar or honey
1 tablespoon fermented black bean paste	1 teaspoon minced garlic
1 tablespoon Shaoxing wine (rice cooking wine)	1 teaspoon minced fresh ginger
1 tablespoon dark soy sauce	1 (680 g) slab baby back ribs, cut into individual ribs

1. In a large bowl, stir together the sesame oil, black bean paste, wine, soy sauce, agave, garlic, and ginger. Add the ribs and toss well to coat. Marinate at room temperature for 30 minutes, or cover and refrigerate for up to 24 hours. 2. Place the ribs in the dual zone; discard the marinade. Set the air fryer to 180°C for 30 minutes.

Sausage and Peppers

Prep time: 7 minutes | Cook time: 35 minutes | Serves 4

Oil, for spraying	1 tablespoon olive oil
900 g hot or sweet Italian-seasoned sausage links, cut into thick slices	1 tablespoon chopped fresh parsley
4 large peppers of any color, seeded and cut into slices	1 teaspoon dried oregano
	1 teaspoon dried basil
1 onion, thinly sliced	1 teaspoon balsamic vinegar

1. Line the air fryer basket with parchment and spray lightly with oil. 2. In a large bowl, combine the sausage, peppers, and onion. 3. In a small bowl, whisk together the olive oil, parsley, oregano, basil, and balsamic vinegar. Pour the mixture over the sausage and peppers and toss until evenly coated. 4. Using a slotted spoon, transfer the mixture to the prepared dual zone air fryer, taking care to drain out as much excess liquid as possible. 5. Air fry at 180°C for 20 minutes, stir, and cook for another 15 minutes, or until the sausage is browned and the juices run clear.

Zesty London Broil

Prep time: 30 minutes | Cook time: 20 to 28 minutes | Serves 4 to 6

160 ml ketchup	2 tablespoons minced onion
60 ml honey	½ teaspoon paprika
60 ml olive oil	1 teaspoon salt
2 tablespoons apple cider vinegar	1 teaspoon freshly ground black pepper
2 tablespoons Worcestershire sauce	900 g bavette or skirt steak (about 1-inch thick)

1. Combine the ketchup, honey, olive oil, apple cider vinegar, Worcestershire sauce, minced onion, paprika, salt and pepper in a small bowl and whisk together. 2. Generously pierce both sides of the meat with a fork or meat tenderizer and place it in a shallow dish. Pour the marinade mixture over the steak, making sure all sides of the meat get coated with the marinade. Cover and refrigerate overnight. 3. Preheat the air fryer to 200°C. 4. Transfer the steak to the dual zone air fryer and air fry for 20 to 28 minutes, depending on how rare or well done you like your steak. Flip the steak over halfway through the cooking time. 5. Remove the steak from the air fryer and let it rest for five minutes on a cutting board. To serve, thinly slice the meat against the grain and transfer to a serving platter.

Herbed Beef

Prep time: 5 minutes | Cook time: 22 minutes | Serves 6

1 teaspoon dried dill	900 g beef steak
1 teaspoon dried thyme	3 tablespoons butter
1 teaspoon garlic powder	

1. Preheat the air fryer to 180°C. 2. Combine the dill, thyme, and garlic powder in a small bowl, and massage into the steak. 3. Air fry the steak in the dual zone air fryer for 20 minutes, then remove, shred, and return to the air fryer. 4. Add the butter and air fry the shredded steak for a further 2 minutes at 190°C. Make sure the beef is coated in the butter before serving.

Lemony Pork Loin Chop Schnitzel

Prep time: 15 minutes | Cook time: 15 minutes | Serves 4

4 thin boneless pork loin chops	235 ml panko breadcrumbs
2 tablespoons lemon juice	2 eggs
120 ml flour	Lemon wedges, for serving
¼ teaspoon marjoram	Cooking spray
1 teaspoon salt	

1. Preheat the air fryer to 180°C and spritz with cooking spray. 2. On a clean work surface, drizzle the pork chops with lemon juice on both sides. 3. Combine the flour with marjoram and salt on a shallow plate. Pour the breadcrumbs on a separate shallow dish. Beat the eggs in a large bowl. 4. Dredge the pork chops in the flour, then dunk in the beaten eggs to coat well. Shake the excess off and roll over the breadcrumbs. 5. Arrange the chops in the preheated dual zone air fryer and spritz with cooking spray. Air fry for 15 minutes or until the chops are golden and crispy. Flip the chops halfway through. Squeeze the lemon wedges over the fried chops and serve immediately.

Blue Cheese Steak Salad

Prep time: 30 minutes | Cook time: 22 minutes | Serves 4

2 tablespoons balsamic vinegar	180 ml extra-virgin olive oil
2 tablespoons red wine vinegar	450 g boneless rump steak
1 tablespoon Dijon mustard	Avocado oil spray
1 tablespoon granulated sweetener	1 small red onion, cut into ¼-inch-thick rounds
1 teaspoon minced garlic	170 g baby spinach
Sea salt and freshly ground black pepper, to taste	120 ml cherry tomatoes, halved
	85 g blue cheese, crumbled

1. In a blender, combine the balsamic vinegar, red wine vinegar, Dijon mustard, sweetener, and garlic. Season with salt and pepper and process until smooth. With the blender running, drizzle in the olive oil. Process until well combined. Transfer to a jar with a tight-fitting lid, and refrigerate until ready to serve (it will keep for up to 2 weeks). 2. Season the steak with salt and pepper and let sit at room temperature for at least 45 minutes, time permitting. 3. Set the air fryer to 200°C. Spray the steak with oil and place it in the dual zone air fryer. Air fry for 6 minutes. Flip the steak and spray it with more oil. Air fry for 6 minutes more for medium-rare or until the steak is done to your liking. 4. Transfer the steak to a plate, tent with a piece of aluminum foil, and allow it to rest. 5. Spray the onion slices with oil and place them in the air fryer basket. Cook at 200°C for 5 minutes. Flip the onion slices and spray them with more oil. Air fry for 5 minutes more. 6. Slice the steak diagonally into thin strips. Place the spinach, cherry tomatoes, onion slices, and steak in a large bowl. Toss with the desired amount of dressing. Sprinkle with crumbled blue cheese and serve.

Cinnamon-Beef Kofta

Prep time: 10 minutes | Cook time: 13 minutes per batch | Makes 12 koftas

680 g lean beef mince	¾ teaspoon salt
1 teaspoon onion granules	¼ teaspoon cayenne
¾ teaspoon ground cinnamon	12 (3½- to 4-inch-long) cinnamon sticks
¾ teaspoon ground dried turmeric	Cooking spray
1 teaspoon ground cumin	

1. Preheat the air fryer to 180°C. Spritz the air fryer basket with cooking spray. 2. Combine all the ingredients, except for the cinnamon sticks, in a large bowl. Toss to mix well. 3. Divide and shape the mixture into 12 balls, then wrap each ball around each cinnamon stick and leave a quarter of the length uncovered. 4. Arrange the beef-cinnamon sticks in the preheated dual zone and spritz with cooking spray. Work in batches to avoid overcrowding. 5. Air fry for 13 minutes or until the beef is browned. Flip the sticks halfway through. 6. Serve immediately.

Spicy Tomato Beef Meatballs

Prep time: 10 minutes | Cook time: 15 minutes | Serves 4

3 spring onions, minced	taste
1 garlic clove, minced	450 g 95% lean beef mince
1 egg yolk	Olive oil spray
60 ml cream cracker crumbs	300 ml any tomato pasta sauce
Pinch salt	2 tablespoons Dijon mustard
Freshly ground black pepper, to	

1. In a large bowl, combine the spring onionspring onions, garlic, egg yolk, cracker crumbs, salt, and pepper and mix well. 2. Add the beef and gently but thoroughly mix with your hands until combined. Form the meat mixture into 1½-inch round meatballs. 3. Insert the crisper plate into the basket and the basket into the unit. Preheat the unit by selecting BAKE, setting the temperature to 200°C, and setting the time to 3 minutes. Select START to begin. 4. Once the unit is preheated, spray the crisper plate with olive oil. Working in batches, spray the meatballs with olive oil and place them into the dual zone in a single layer, without touching. 5. Select BAKE, set the temperature to 200°C, and set the time to 11 minutes. Select START to begin. 6. When the cooking is complete, a food thermometer inserted into the meatballs should register 74°C. Transfer the meatballs to a 6-inch metal bowl. 7. Repeat steps 4, 5, and 6 with the remaining meatballs. 8. Top the meatballs with the pasta sauce and Dijon mustard, and mix gently. Place the bowl into the dual zone. 9. Select BAKE, set the temperature to 200°C, and set the time to 4 minutes. Select START to begin. 10. When the cooking is complete, serve hot.

Vietnamese Grilled Pork

Prep time: 30 minutes | Cook time: 20 minutes | Serves 6

60 ml minced brown onion	½ teaspoon black pepper
2 tablespoons sugar	680 g boneless pork shoulder, cut into ½-inch-thick slices
2 tablespoons vegetable oil	60 ml chopped salted roasted peanuts
1 tablespoon minced garlic	
1 tablespoon fish sauce	2 tablespoons chopped fresh coriander or parsley
1 tablespoon minced fresh lemongrass	
2 teaspoons dark soy sauce	

1. In a large bowl, combine the onion, sugar, vegetable oil, garlic, fish sauce, lemongrass, soy sauce, and pepper. Add the pork and toss to coat. Marinate at room temperature for 30 minutes, or cover and refrigerate for up to 24 hours. 2. Arrange the pork slices in the dual zone air fryer; discard the marinade. Set the air fryer to 200°C for 20 minutes, turning the pork halfway through the cooking time. 3. Transfer the pork to a serving platter. Sprinkle with the peanuts and coriander and serve.

Pork and Tricolor Vegetables Kebabs

Prep time: 1 hour 20 minutes | Cook time: 8 minutes per batch | Serves 4

For the Pork:
450 g pork steak, cut in cubes
1 tablespoon white wine vinegar
3 tablespoons steak sauce or brown sauce
60 ml soy sauce
1 teaspoon powdered chili
1 teaspoon red chili flakes
2 teaspoons smoked paprika
1 teaspoon garlic salt
For the Vegetable:
1 courgette, cut in cubes
1 butternut squash, deseeded and cut in cubes
1 red pepper, cut in cubes
1 green pepper, cut in cubes
Salt and ground black pepper, to taste
Cooking spray
Special Equipment:
4 bamboo skewers, soaked in water for at least 30 minutes

1. Combine the ingredients for the pork in a large bowl. Press the pork to dunk in the marinade. Wrap the bowl in plastic and refrigerate for at least an hour. 2. Preheat the air fryer to 190°C and spritz with cooking spray. 3. Remove the pork from the marinade and run the skewers through the pork and vegetables alternatively. Sprinkle with salt and pepper to taste. 4. Arrange the skewers in the preheated dual zone air fryer and spritz with cooking spray. Air fry for 8 minutes or until the pork is browned and the vegetables are lightly charred and tender. Flip the skewers halfway through. You may need to work in batches to avoid overcrowding. 5. Serve immediately.

Greek-Style Meatloaf

Prep time: 5 minutes | Cook time: 25 minutes | Serves 6

450 g lean beef mince
2 eggs
2 plum tomatoes, diced
½ brown onion, diced
120 ml whole wheat bread crumbs
1 teaspoon garlic powder
1 teaspoon dried oregano
1 teaspoon dried thyme
1 teaspoon salt
1 teaspoon black pepper
60 g mozzarella cheese, shredded
1 tablespoon olive oil
Fresh chopped parsley, for garnish

1. Preheat the oven to 190°C. 2. In a large bowl, mix together the beef, eggs, tomatoes, onion, bread crumbs, garlic powder, oregano, thyme, salt, pepper, and cheese. 3. Form into a loaf, flattening to 1-inch thick. 4. Brush the top with olive oil, then place the meatloaf into the dual zone air fryer and cook for 25 minutes. 5. Remove from the air fryer and allow to rest for 5 minutes, before slicing and serving with a sprinkle of parsley.

Pork Bulgogi

Prep time: 30 minutes | Cook time: 15 minutes | Serves 4

1 onion, thinly sliced
2 tablespoons gochujang (Korean red chili paste)
1 tablespoon minced fresh ginger
1 tablespoon minced garlic
1 tablespoon soy sauce
1 tablespoon Shaoxing wine (rice cooking wine)
1 tablespoon toasted sesame oil
1 teaspoon sugar
¼ to 1 teaspoon cayenne pepper or gochugaru (Korean ground red pepper)
450 g boneless pork shoulder, cut into ½-inch-thick slices
1 tablespoon sesame seeds
60 ml sliced spring onionspring onions

1. In a large bowl, combine the onion, gochujang, ginger, garlic, soy sauce, wine, sesame oil, sugar, and cayenne. Add the pork and toss to coat. Marinate at room temperature for 30 minutes, or cover and refrigerate for up to 24 hours. 2. Arrange the pork and onion slices in dual zone the air fryer; discard the marinade. Set the air fryer to 200°C for 15 minutes, turning the pork halfway through the cooking time. 3. Arrange the pork on a serving platter. Sprinkle with the sesame seeds and spring onionspring onions and serve.

Air Fried Beef Satay with Peanut Dipping Sauce

Prep time: 30 minutes | Cook time: 5 to 7 minutes | Serves 4

230 g bavette or skirt steak, sliced into 8 strips
2 teaspoons curry powder
½ teaspoon coarse or flaky salt
Cooking spray
Peanut Dipping sauce:
2 tablespoons creamy peanut butter
1 tablespoon reduced-salt soy sauce
2 teaspoons rice vinegar
1 teaspoon honey
1 teaspoon grated ginger
Special Equipment:
4 bamboo skewers, cut into halves and soaked in water for 20 minutes to keep them from burning while cooking

1. Preheat the air fryer to 180°C. Spritz the air fryer basket with cooking spray. 2. In a bowl, place the steak strips and sprinkle with the curry powder and coarse or flaky salt to season. Thread the strips onto the soaked skewers. 3. Arrange the skewers in the prepared dual zone air fryer and spritz with cooking spray. Air fry for 5 to 7 minutes, or until the beef is well browned, turning halfway through. 4. In the meantime, stir together the peanut butter, soy sauce, rice vinegar, honey, and ginger in a bowl to make the dipping sauce. 5. Transfer the beef to the serving dishes and let rest for 5 minutes. Serve with the peanut dipping sauce on the side.

Sweet and Spicy Country-Style Ribs

Prep time: 10 minutes | Cook time: 25 minutes | Serves 4

- 2 tablespoons brown sugar
- 2 tablespoons smoked paprika
- 1 teaspoon garlic powder
- 1 teaspoon onion granules
- 1 teaspoon mustard powder
- 1 teaspoon ground cumin
- 1 teaspoon coarse or flaky salt
- 1 teaspoon black pepper
- ¼ to ½ teaspoon cayenne pepper
- 680 g boneless pork steaks
- 235 ml barbecue sauce

1. In a small bowl, stir together the brown sugar, paprika, garlic powder, onion granules, mustard powder, cumin, salt, black pepper, and cayenne. Mix until well combined. 2. Pat the ribs dry with a paper towel. Generously sprinkle the rub evenly over both sides of the ribs and rub in with your fingers. 3. Place the ribs in the dual zone air fryer. Set the air fryer to 180°C for 15 minutes. Turn the ribs and brush with 120 ml of the barbecue sauce. Cook for an additional 10 minutes. Use a meat thermometer to ensure the pork has reached an internal temperature of 64°C. 4. Serve with remaining barbecue sauce.

Bacon, Cheese and Pear Stuffed Pork

Prep time: 10 minutes | Cook time: 24 minutes | Serves 3

- 4 slices bacon, chopped
- 1 tablespoon butter
- 120 ml finely diced onion
- 80 ml chicken stock
- 355 ml seasoned stuffing mix
- 1 egg, beaten
- ½ teaspoon dried thyme
- ½ teaspoon salt
- ⅛ teaspoon black pepper
- 1 pear, finely diced
- 80 ml crumbled blue cheese
- 3 boneless pork chops (2-inch thick)
- Olive oil
- Salt and freshly ground black pepper, to taste

1. Preheat the air fryer to 200°C. 2. Place the bacon into the zone 1 air fryer and air fry for 6 minutes, stirring halfway through the cooking time. Remove the bacon and set it aside on a paper towel. Pour out the grease from the bottom of the air fryer. 3. Make the stuffing: Melt the butter in a medium saucepan over medium heat on the stovetop. Add the onion and sauté for a few minutes, until it starts to soften. Add the chicken stock and simmer for 1 minute. Remove the pan from the heat and add the stuffing mix. Stir until the stock has been absorbed. Add the egg, dried thyme, salt and freshly ground black pepper, and stir until combined. Fold in the diced pear and crumbled blue cheese. 4. Place the pork chops on a cutting board. Using the palm of your hand to hold the chop flat and steady, slice into the side of the pork chop to make a pocket in the center of the chop. Leave about an inch of chop uncut and make sure you don't cut all the way through the pork chop. Brush both sides of the pork chops with olive oil and season with salt and freshly ground black pepper. Stuff each pork chop with a third of the stuffing, packing the stuffing tightly inside the pocket. 5. Preheat the air fryer to 180°C. 6. Spray or brush the sides of the dual zone air fryer with oil. Place the pork chops in the air fryer basket with the open stuffed edge of the pork chop facing the outside edges of the basket. 7. Air fry the pork chops for 18 minutes, turning the pork chops over halfway through the cooking time. When the chops are done, let them rest for 5 minutes and then transfer to a serving platter.

Italian Pork Loin

Prep time: 30 minutes | Cook time: 16 minutes | Serves 3

- 1 teaspoon sea salt
- ½ teaspoon black pepper, freshly cracked
- 60 ml red wine
- 2 tablespoons mustard
- 2 garlic cloves, minced
- 450 g pork loin joint
- 1 tablespoon Italian herb seasoning blend

1. In a ceramic bowl, mix the salt, black pepper, red wine, mustard, and garlic. Add the pork loin and let it marinate at least 30 minutes. 2. Spritz the sides and bottom of the air fryer basket with nonstick cooking spray. 3. Place the pork loin in the dual zone; sprinkle with the Italian herb seasoning blend. Cook the pork loin at 190°C for 10 minutes. Select AIR FRY. Select START. Flip halfway through, spraying with cooking oil and cook for 5 to 6 minutes more. Serve immediately.

Mozzarella Stuffed Beef and Pork Meatballs

Prep time: 15 minutes | Cook time: 12 minutes | Serves 4 to 6

- 1 tablespoon olive oil
- 1 small onion, finely chopped
- 1 to 2 cloves garlic, minced
- 340 g beef mince
- 340 g pork mince
- 180 ml bread crumbs
- 60 ml grated Parmesan cheese
- 60 ml finely chopped fresh parsley
- ½ teaspoon dried oregano
- 1½ teaspoons salt
- Freshly ground black pepper, to taste
- 2 eggs, lightly beaten
- 140 g low-moisture Mozzarella or other melting cheese, cut into 1-inch cubes

1. Preheat a skillet over medium-high heat. Add the oil and cook the onion and garlic until tender, but not browned. 2. Transfer the onion and garlic to a large bowl and add the beef, pork, bread crumbs, Parmesan cheese, parsley, oregano, salt, pepper and eggs. Mix well until all the ingredients are combined. Divide the mixture into 12 evenly sized balls. Make one meatball at a time, by pressing a hole in the meatball mixture with the finger and pushing a piece of Mozzarella cheese into the hole. Mold the meat back into a ball, enclosing the cheese. 3. Preheat the air fryer to 190°C. 4. Working in two batches, transfer six of the meatballs to the dual zone air fryer basket and air fry for 12 minutes, shaking the basket and turning the meatballs twice during the cooking process. Repeat with the remaining 6 meatballs. Serve warm.

Marinated Steak Tips with Mushrooms

Prep time: 30 minutes | Cook time: 10 minutes | Serves 4

680 g rump steak, trimmed and cut into 1-inch pieces	1 tablespoon olive oil
230 g brown mushrooms, halved	1 teaspoon paprika
	1 teaspoon crushed red pepper flakes
60 ml Worcestershire sauce	2 tablespoons chopped fresh parsley (optional)
1 tablespoon Dijon mustard	

1. Place the beef and mushrooms in a gallon-size resealable bag. In a small bowl, whisk together the Worcestershire, mustard, olive oil, paprika, and red pepper flakes. Pour the marinade into the bag and massage gently to ensure the beef and mushrooms are evenly coated. Seal the bag and refrigerate for at least 4 hours, preferably overnight. Remove from the refrigerator 30 minutes before cooking. 2. Preheat the air fryer to 200°C. 3. Drain and discard the marinade. Arrange the steak and mushrooms in the dual zone. Air fry for 10 minutes, pausing halfway through the baking time to shake the basket. Transfer to a serving plate and top with the parsley, if desired.

Mustard Herb Pork Tenderloin

Prep time: 5 minutes | Cook time: 20 minutes | Serves 6

60 ml mayonnaise	1 (450 g) pork tenderloin
2 tablespoons Dijon mustard	½ teaspoon salt
½ teaspoon dried thyme	¼ teaspoon ground black pepper
¼ teaspoon dried rosemary	

1. In a small bowl, mix mayonnaise, mustard, thyme, and rosemary. Brush tenderloin with mixture on all sides, then sprinkle with salt and pepper on all sides. 2. Place tenderloin into ungreased dual zone. Adjust the temperature to 200°C and air fry for 20 minutes, turning tenderloin halfway through cooking. Tenderloin will be golden and have an internal temperature of at least 64°C when done. Serve warm.

Garlic-Marinated Bavette Steak

Prep time: 30 minutes | Cook time: 8 to 10 minutes | Serves 6

120 ml avocado oil	1½ teaspoons sea salt
60 ml soy sauce or tamari	1 teaspoon freshly ground black pepper
1 shallot, minced	
1 tablespoon minced garlic	¼ teaspoon red pepper flakes
2 tablespoons chopped fresh oregano, or 2 teaspoons dried	900 g bavette or skirt steak

1. In a blender, combine the avocado oil, soy sauce, shallot, garlic, oregano, salt, black pepper, and red pepper flakes. Process until smooth. 2. Place the steak in a zip-top plastic bag or shallow dish with the marinade. Seal the bag or cover the dish and marinate in the refrigerator for at least 2 hours or overnight. 3. Remove the steak from the bag and discard the marinade. 4. Set the air fryer to 200°C. Place the steak in the dual zone (if needed, cut into sections and work in batches). Air fry for 4 to 6 minutes, flip the steak, and cook for another 4 minutes or until the internal temperature reaches 49°C in the thickest part for medium-rare (or as desired).

Pork Medallions with Endive Salad

Prep time: 25 minutes | Cook time: 7 minutes | Serves 4

1 (230 g) pork tenderloin	honey or maple syrup)
Salt and freshly ground black pepper, to taste	1 tablespoon Dijon mustard
	juice of ½ lemon
60 ml flour	2 tablespoons chopped chervil or flat-leaf parsley
2 eggs, lightly beaten	
180 ml finely crushed crackers	salt and freshly ground black pepper
1 teaspoon paprika	
1 teaspoon mustard powder	120 ml extra-virgin olive oil
1 teaspoon garlic powder	Endive Salad:
1 teaspoon dried thyme	1 heart romaine lettuce, torn into large pieces
1 teaspoon salt	
vegetable or rapeseed oil, in spray bottle	2 heads endive, sliced
	120 ml cherry tomatoes, halved
Vinaigrette:	85 g fresh Mozzarella, diced
60 ml white balsamic vinegar	Salt and freshly ground black pepper, to taste
2 tablespoons agave syrup (or	

1. Slice the pork tenderloin into 1-inch slices. Using a meat pounder, pound the pork slices into thin ½-inch medallions. Generously season the pork with salt and freshly ground black pepper on both sides. 2. Set up a dredging station using three shallow dishes. Put the flour in one dish and the beaten eggs in a second dish. Combine the crushed crackers, paprika, mustard powder, garlic powder, thyme and salt in a third dish. 3. Preheat the air fryer to 200°C. 4. Dredge the pork medallions in flour first and then into the beaten egg. Let the excess egg drip off and coat both sides of the medallions with the cracker crumb mixture. Spray both sides of the coated medallions with vegetable or rapeseed oil. 5. Air fry the medallions in two batches in the dual zone at 200°C for 5 minutes. Once you have air-fried all the medallions, flip them all over. Air fry at 200°C for an additional 2 minutes. 6. While the medallions are cooking, make the salad and dressing. Whisk the white balsamic vinegar, agave syrup, Dijon mustard, lemon juice, chervil, salt and pepper together in a small bowl. Whisk in the olive oil slowly until combined and thickened. 7. Combine the romaine lettuce, endive, cherry tomatoes, and Mozzarella cheese in a large salad bowl. Drizzle the dressing over the vegetables and toss to combine. Season with salt and freshly ground black pepper. 8. Serve the pork medallions warm on or beside the salad.

Bean and Beef Meatball Taco Pizza

Prep time: 10 minutes | Cook time: 7 to 9 minutes per batch | Serves 4

180 ml refried beans (from a 450 g can)
120 ml salsa
10 frozen precooked beef meatballs, thawed and sliced
1 jalapeño pepper, sliced
4 whole-wheat pitta breads
235 ml shredded chilli cheese
120 ml shredded Monterey Jack or Cheddar cheese
Cooking oil spray
80 ml sour cream

1. In a medium bowl, stir together the refried beans, salsa, meatballs, and jalapeño. 2. Insert the crisper plate into the basket and the basket into the unit. Preheat the unit by selecting BAKE, setting the temperature to 190°C, and setting the time to 3 minutes. Select START to begin. 3. Top the pittas with the refried bean mixture and sprinkle with the cheeses. 4. Once the unit is preheated, spray the crisper plate with cooking oil. Working in batches, place the pizzas into the dual zone. Select BAKE, set the temperature to 190°C, and set the time to 9 minutes. Select START to begin. 5. After about 7 minutes, check the pizzas. They are done when the cheese is melted and starts to brown. If not ready, resume cooking. 6. When the cooking is complete, top each pizza with a dollop of sour cream and serve warm.

Simple Beef Mince with Courgette

Prep time: 5 minutes | Cook time: 12 minutes | Serves 4

680 g beef mince
450 g chopped courgette
2 tablespoons extra-virgin olive oil
1 teaspoon dried oregano
1 teaspoon dried basil
1 teaspoon dried rosemary
2 tablespoons fresh chives, chopped

1. Preheat the air fryer to 180°C. 2. In a large bowl, combine all the ingredients, except for the chives, until well blended. 3. Place the beef and courgette mixture in the dual zone baking pan. Air fry for 12 minutes, or until the beef is browned and the courgette is tender. 4. Divide the beef and courgette mixture among four serving dishes. Top with fresh chives and serve hot.

Chapter 6 Fish and Seafood

Chapter 6 Fish and Seafood

Garlic Lemon Scallops

Prep time: 5 minutes | Cook time: 10 minutes | Serves 4

4 tablespoons salted butter, melted
4 teaspoons peeled and finely minced garlic
½ small lemon, zested and juiced
8 sea scallops, 30 g each, cleaned and patted dry
¼ teaspoon salt
¼ teaspoon ground black pepper

1. In a small bowl, mix butter, garlic, lemon zest, and lemon juice. Place scallops in an ungreased round nonstick baking dish. Pour butter mixture over scallops, then sprinkle with salt and pepper. 2. Place dish into dual zone air fryer. Adjust the temperature to 180°C and bake for 10 minutes. Scallops will be opaque and firm, and have an internal temperature of 56°C when done. Serve warm.

Simple Buttery Cod

Prep time: 5 minutes | Cook time: 8 minutes | Serves 2

2 cod fillets, 110 g each
2 tablespoons salted butter, melted
1 teaspoon Old Bay seasoning
½ medium lemon, sliced

1. Place cod fillets into a round baking dish. Brush each fillet with butter and sprinkle with Old Bay seasoning. Lay two lemon slices on each fillet. Cover the dish with foil and place into the dual zone air fryer basket. 2. Adjust the temperature to 180°C and bake for 8 minutes. Flip halfway through the cooking time. When cooked, internal temperature should be at least 64°C. Serve warm.

Tuna-Stuffed Quinoa Patties

Prep time: 10 minutes | Cook time: 15 minutes | Serves 4

35 g quinoa
4 slices white bread with crusts removed
120 ml milk
3 eggs
280 g tuna packed in olive oil, drained
2 to 3 lemons
Kosher or coarse sea salt, and pepper, to taste
150 g panko bread crumbs
Vegetable oil, for spraying
Lemon wedges, for serving

1. Rinse the quinoa in a fine-mesh sieve until the water runs clear. Bring 1 liter of salted water to a boil. Add the quinoa, cover, and reduce heat to low. Simmer the quinoa covered until most of the water is absorbed and the quinoa is tender, 15 to 20 minutes. Drain and allow to cool to room temperature. Meanwhile, soak the bread in the milk. 2. Mix the drained quinoa with the soaked bread and 2 of the eggs in a large bowl and mix thoroughly. In a medium bowl, combine the tuna, the remaining egg, and the juice and zest of 1 of the lemons. Season well with salt and pepper. Spread the panko on a plate. 3. Scoop up approximately 60 g of the quinoa mixture and flatten into a patty. Place a heaping tablespoon of the tuna mixture in the center of the patty and close the quinoa around the tuna. Flatten the patty slightly to create an oval-shaped croquette. Dredge both sides of the croquette in the panko. Repeat with the remaining quinoa and tuna. 4. Spray the dual zone air fryer with oil to prevent sticking, and preheat the air fryer to 200°C. Arrange 4 or 5 of the croquettes in the every single zone, taking care to avoid overcrowding. Spray the tops of the croquettes with oil. Air fry for 8 minutes until the top side is browned and crispy. Carefully turn the croquettes over and spray the second side with oil. Air fry until the second side is browned and crispy, another 7 minutes. Repeat with the remaining croquettes. 5. Serve the croquetas warm with plenty of lemon wedges for spritzing.

Salmon with Provolone Cheese and Prawn Bake

Prep time: 20 minutes | Cook time: 15 minutes | Serves 4

Salmon with Provolone Cheese:
455 g salmon fillet, chopped
60 g Provolone or Edam, grated
1 teaspoon avocado oil
¼ teaspoon ground paprika
Prawn Bake:
400 g prawns, peeled and deveined
1 egg, beaten
120 ml coconut milk
120 g Cheddar cheese, shredded
½ teaspoon coconut oil
1 teaspoon ground coriander

1. Sprinkle the salmon fillets with avocado oil and put in the dual zone air fryer. 2. Then sprinkle the fish with ground paprika and top with Provolone cheese. 3. In the mixing bowl, mix prawns with egg, coconut milk, Cheddar cheese, coconut oil, and ground coriander. 4. Then put the mixture in the baking ramekins and put in the zone 2. 5. Cook the prawns at 200°C for 5 minutes. 6. Cook the fish at 180°C for 15 minutes.

Salmon Fritters with Courgette and Blackened Fish

Prep time: 30 minutes | Cook time: 12 minutes | Serves 4

Salmon Fritters with Courgette:	pepper
2 tablespoons almond flour	Blackened Fish:
1 courgette, grated	1 large egg, beaten
1 egg, beaten	Blackened seasoning, as needed
170 g salmon fillet, diced	2 tablespoons light brown sugar
1 teaspoon avocado oil	4 tilapia fillets, 110g each
½ teaspoon ground black	Cooking spray

1. Preheat the air fryer to 180°C. Mix almond flour with courgette, egg, salmon, and ground black pepper. 2. Then make the fritters from the salmon mixture. 3. Sprinkle the zone 1 with avocado oil and put the fritters inside. 4. In a shallow bowl, place the beaten egg. In a second shallow bowl, stir together the Blackened seasoning and the brown sugar. 5. One at a time, dip the fish fillets in the egg, then the brown sugar mixture, coating thoroughly. 6. Line the zone 1 with baking paper. Place the coated fish on the baking paper in the zone 2 and spritz with oil. 7. Set the temperature to 190°C for 6 minutes per side and Select AIR FRY for the zone 1. Set the temperature to 200°C for 4 minutes and select BAKE. Select START. Flip the fish, spritz it with oil, and bake for 4 to 6 minutes more until the fish is white inside and flakes easily with a fork. 8. Serve immediately.

Mouthwatering Cod over Creamy Leek Noodles

Prep time: 10 minutes | Cook time: 24 minutes | Serves 4

1 small leek, sliced into long thin noodles	Coating:
120 ml heavy cream	20 g grated Parmesan cheese
2 cloves garlic, minced	2 tablespoons mayonnaise
1 teaspoon fine sea salt, divided	2 tablespoons unsalted butter, softened
4 cod fillets, 110 g each (about 1 inch thick)	1 tablespoon chopped fresh thyme, or ½ teaspoon dried thyme leaves, plus more for garnish
½ teaspoon ground black pepper	

1. Preheat the air fryer to 180°C. 2. Place the leek noodles in a casserole dish or a pan that will fit in your air fryer. 3. In a small bowl, stir together the cream, garlic, and ½ teaspoon of the salt. Pour the mixture over the leeks and cook in the zone 1 air fryer for 10 minutes, or until the leeks are very tender. 4. Pat the fish dry and season with the remaining ½ teaspoon of salt and the pepper. When the leeks are ready, open the zone 2 air fryer and place the fish fillets on top of the leeks. Air fry for 8 to 10 minutes, until the fish flakes easily with a fork (the thicker the fillets, the longer this will take). 5. While the fish cooks, make the coating: In a small bowl, combine the Parmesan, mayo, butter, and thyme. 6. When the fish is ready, remove it from the air fryer and increase the heat to 218°C (or as high as your air fryer can go). Spread the fillets with a ½-inch-thick to ¾-inch-thick layer of the coating. 7. Place the fish back in the dual zone air fryer and air fry for 3 to 4 minutes, until the coating browns. 8. Garnish with fresh or dried thyme, if desired. Store leftovers in an airtight container in the refrigerator for up to 3 days. Reheat in a casserole dish in a preheated 180°C air fryer for 6 minutes, or until heated through.

Cucumber and Salmon Salad and Roasted Halibut Steaks with Parsley

Prep time: 15 minutes | Cook time: 10 minutes

Cucumber and Salmon Salad | Serves 2:	Roasted Halibut Steaks with Parsley | Serves 4:
455 g salmon fillet	455 g halibut steaks
1½ tablespoons olive oil, divided	60 ml vegetable oil
1 tablespoon sherry vinegar	2½ tablespoons Worcester sauce
1 tablespoon capers, rinsed and drained	2 tablespoons honey
1 seedless cucumber, thinly sliced	2 tablespoons vermouth or white wine vinegar
¼ white onion, thinly sliced	1 tablespoon freshly squeezed lemon juice
2 tablespoons chopped fresh parsley	1 tablespoon fresh parsley leaves, coarsely chopped
Salt and freshly ground black pepper, to taste	Salt and pepper, to taste
	1 teaspoon dried basil

1. Preheat the air fryer to 180°C. 2. Lightly coat the salmon with ½ tablespoon of the olive oil. Place skin-side down in the zone 1. 2. Put all the ingredients in a large mixing dish and gently stir until the fish is coated evenly. Transfer the fish to the zone 2. Set the temperature 200°. Set the time to 8 to 10 minutes and AIR FRY for the zone 1 until the fish is opaque and flakes easily with a fork. Set the time to 10 minutes and ROAST. Select START. 3. Transfer the salmon to a plate and let cool to room temperature. Remove the skin and carefully flake the fish into bite-size chunks. flipping the fish halfway through, or until the fish reaches an internal temperature of at least 64°C on a meat thermometer. 4. In a small bowl, whisk the remaining 1 tablespoon olive oil and the vinegar until thoroughly combined. Add the flaked fish, capers, cucumber, onion, and parsley. Season to taste with salt and freshly ground black pepper. Toss gently to coat. Serve immediately or cover and refrigerate for up to 4 hours. 5. Let the fish cool for 5 minutes and serve.

Popcorn Prawns

Prep time: 15 minutes | Cook time: 18 to 20 minutes | Serves 4

70 g plain flour, plus 2 tablespoons
½ teaspoon garlic powder
1½ teaspoons Old Bay Seasoning
½ teaspoon onion powder
120 ml beer, plus 2 tablespoons
340 g prawns, peeled and deveined
Olive oil for misting or cooking spray
Coating:
180 g panko crumbs
1 teaspoon Old Bay Seasoning
½ teaspoon ground black pepper

1. In a large bowl, mix together the flour, garlic powder, Old Bay Seasoning, and onion powder. Stir in beer to blend. 2. Add prawns to batter and stir to coat. 3. Combine the coating ingredients in food processor and pulse to finely crush the crumbs. Transfer crumbs to shallow dish. 4. Preheat the air fryer to 200°C. 5. Pour the prawns and batter into a colander to drain. Stir with a spoon to drain excess batter. 6. Working with a handful of prawns at a time, roll in crumbs and place on a cookie sheet. 7. Spray breaded prawns with oil or cooking spray and place all at once into dual zone air fryer. 8. Air fry for 5 minutes. Shake basket or stir and mist again with olive oil or spray. Cook 5 more minutes, shake basket again, and mist lightly again. Continue cooking 3 to 5 more minutes, until browned and crispy.

Ahi Tuna Steaks and Foil-Packet Lobster Tail

Prep time: 20 minutes | Cook time: 14 minutes | Serves 2

Ahi Tuna Steaks:
2 ahi tuna steaks, 170g each
2 tablespoons olive oil
3 tablespoons everything bagel seasoning
Foil-Packet Lobster Tail:
2 lobster tails, 170 g each halved
2 tablespoons salted butter, melted
½ teaspoon Old Bay seasoning
Juice of ½ medium lemon
1 teaspoon dried parsley

1. Drizzle both sides of each steak with olive oil. Place seasoning on a medium plate and press each side of tuna steaks into seasoning to form a thick layer. 2. Seal the foil packets, completely covering tails. Place into the zone 2. Place steaks into ungreased zone 1. 3. Set the temperature to 200°C and the time to 14 minutes for the zone 1. Set the temperature to 190°C and the time to 12 minutes for the zone 2. Select AIR FRY. Select START, turning steaks halfway through cooking. Steaks will be done when internal temperature is at least 64°C for well-done. 4. Place the two halved tails on a sheet of aluminum foil. Drizzle with butter, Old Bay seasoning, and lemon juice. 5. Once done, sprinkle with dried parsley and serve immediately.

Cheesy Tuna Patties and Sea Bass with Potato Scales

Prep time: 15 minutes | Cook time: 18 minutes

Cheesy Tuna Patties | Serves 4:
Tuna Patties:
455 g canned tuna, drained
1 egg, whisked
2 tablespoons shallots, minced
1 garlic clove, minced
1 cup grated Romano cheese
Sea salt and ground black pepper, to taste
1 tablespoon sesame oil
Cheese Sauce:
1 tablespoon butter
240 ml beer
2 tablespoons grated Cheddar cheese
Sea Bass with Potato Scales | Serves 2:
2 fillets of sea bass, 170- to 230 g each
Salt and freshly ground black pepper, to taste
60 ml mayonnaise
2 teaspoons finely chopped lemon zest
1 teaspoon chopped fresh thyme
2 Fingerling, or new potatoes, very thinly sliced into rounds
Olive oil
½ clove garlic, crushed into a paste
1 tablespoon capers, drained and rinsed
1 tablespoon olive oil
1 teaspoon lemon juice, to taste

1. Preheat the air fryer to 180°C. Mix together the canned tuna, whisked egg, shallots, garlic, cheese, salt, and pepper in a large bowl and stir to incorporate. 2. Divide the tuna mixture into four equal portions and form each portion into a patty with your hands. Refrigerate the patties for 2 hours. 3. When ready, brush both sides of each patty with sesame oil. 4. Season the fish well with salt and freshly ground black pepper. Mix the mayonnaise, lemon zest and thyme together in a small bowl. Spread a thin layer of the mayonnaise mixture on both fillets. Start layering rows of potato slices onto the fish fillets to simulate the fish scales. The second row should overlap the first row slightly. Dabbing a little more mayonnaise along the upper edge of the row of potatoes where the next row overlaps will help the potato slices stick. Press the potatoes onto the fish to secure them well and season again with salt. Brush or spray the potato layer with olive oil. 5. Place the patties in the zone 1. Meanwhile, melt the butter in a pan over medium heat. 6. Pour in the beer and whisk constantly, or until it begins to bubble. 7. Add the grated Colby cheese and mix well. Put the patties in the zone 1. Transfer the fish to the zone 2. 8. Set the temperature to 200°C. Set the time to 14 minutes for the zone 1 and 8 to 10 minutes for the zone 2. Select AIR FRY. Select START, flipping the patties halfway through, or until lightly browned and cooked through. Continue cooking for 3 to 4 minutes, or until the cheese melts. Remove the patties from the basket to a plate. Drizzle them with the cheese sauce and serve immediately. 9. While the fish is cooking, add the garlic, capers, olive oil and lemon juice to the remaining mayonnaise mixture to make the caper aïoli. 10. Serve the fish warm with a dollop of the aïoli on top or on the side.

Classic Fish Sticks with Tartar Sauce

Prep time: 10 minutes | Cook time: 12 to 15 minutes | Serves 4

680 g cod fillets, cut into 1-inch strips	120 ml sour cream
1 teaspoon salt	120 ml mayonnaise
½ teaspoon freshly ground black pepper	3 tablespoons chopped dill pickle
2 eggs	2 tablespoons capers, drained and chopped
70 g almond flour	½ teaspoon dried dill
20 g grated Parmesan cheese	1 tablespoon dill pickle liquid (optional)
Tartar Sauce:	

1. Preheat the air fryer to 180°C. 2. Season the cod with the salt and black pepper; set aside. 3. In a shallow bowl, lightly beat the eggs. In a second shallow bowl, combine the almond flour and Parmesan cheese. Stir until thoroughly combined. 4. Working with a few pieces at a time, dip the fish into the egg mixture followed by the flour mixture. Press lightly to ensure an even coating. 5. Working in batches if necessary, arrange the fish in a single layer in the dual zone air fryer and spray lightly with olive oil. Pausing halfway through the cooking time to turn the fish, air fry for 12 to 15 minutes, until the fish flakes easily with a fork. Let sit in the basket for a few minutes before serving with the tartar sauce. 6. To make the tartar sauce: In a small bowl, combine the sour cream, mayonnaise, pickle, capers, and dill. If you prefer a thinner sauce, stir in the pickle liquid.

Oyster Po'Boy and Crunchy Fish Sticks

Prep time: 50 minutes | Cook time: 9 minutes | Serves 4

Oyster Po'Boy:	Cooking spray
105 g plain flour	Crunchy Fish Sticks:
40 g yellow cornmeal	455 g cod fillets
1 tablespoon Cajun seasoning	170 g finely ground blanched almond flour
1 teaspoon salt	2 teaspoons Old Bay seasoning
2 large eggs, beaten	½ teaspoon paprika
1 teaspoon hot sauce	Sea salt and freshly ground black pepper, to taste
455 g pre-shucked oysters	60 ml mayonnaise
1 (12-inch) French baguette, quartered and sliced horizontally	1 large egg, beaten
Tartar Sauce, as needed	Avocado oil spray
150 g shredded lettuce, divided	Tartar sauce, for serving
2 tomatoes, cut into slices	

1. Preheat the air fryer to 180°C. In a shallow bowl, whisk the flour, cornmeal, Cajun seasoning, and salt until blended. In a second shallow bowl, whisk together the eggs and hot sauce. 2. One at a time, dip the oysters in the cornmeal mixture, the eggs, and again in the cornmeal, coating thoroughly. 3. Line the zone 1 with baking paper. 4. Place the oysters on the zone 1 and spritz with oil. 5. Cut the fish into ¾-inch-wide strips. 6. In a shallow bowl, stir together the almond flour, Old Bay seasoning, paprika, and salt and pepper to taste. In another shallow bowl, whisk together the mayonnaise and egg. 7. Dip the cod strips in the egg mixture, then the almond flour, gently pressing with your fingers to help adhere to the coating. 8. Place the coated fish on a baking paper-lined baking sheet and freeze for 30 minutes. 9. Spray the zone 2 with oil. 10. Place the fish in the zone 2 in a single layer, and spray each piece with oil. Set the temperature to 200°C. Set the time to 2 minutes for the zone 1 and 5 minutes for the zone 2. Select AIR FRY. Select START. Shake the basket, spritz the oysters with oil, and air fry for 3 minutes more until lightly browned and crispy. 11. Flip and spray with more oil. Cook for 4 minutes more, until the internal temperature reaches 60°C. Serve with the tartar sauce. 12. Spread each sandwich half with Tartar Sauce. Assemble the po'boys by layering each sandwich with fried oysters, ½ cup shredded lettuce, and 2 tomato slices. 7. Serve immediately.

Pecan-Crusted Catfish and Crab Legs

Prep time: 10 minutes | Cook time: 15 minutes | Serves 4

Pecan-Crusted Catfish:	Pecan halves
65 g pecans, finely crushed	Crab Legs:
1 teaspoon fine sea salt	60 g salted butter, melted and divided
¼ teaspoon ground black pepper	1.4 kg crab legs
4 catfish fillets, 110g each	¼ teaspoon garlic powder
For Garnish (Optional):	Juice of ½ medium lemon
Fresh oregano	

1. Preheat the air fryer to 180°C. Spray the air fryer basket with avocado oil. 2. In a large bowl, mix the crushed pecan, salt, and pepper. One at a time, dredge the catfish fillets in the mixture, coating them well. Use your hands to press the pecan meal into the fillets. Spray the fish with avocado oil and place them in the zone 1. 3. In a large bowl, drizzle 2 tablespoons butter over crab legs. Place crab legs into the zone 2. 4. Adjust the temperature to 200°C and air fry for 15 minutes. 5. Air fry the coated catfish for 12 minutes, or until it flakes easily and is no longer translucent in the center, flipping halfway through. 6. Garnish with oregano sprigs and pecan halves, if desired. 7. Store leftovers in an airtight container in the fridge for up to 3 days. Reheat in a preheated 180°C air fryer for 4 minutes, or until heated through. 8. Shake the air fryer basket to toss the crab legs halfway through the cooking time. 9. In a small bowl, mix remaining butter, garlic powder, and lemon juice. 10. To serve, crack open crab legs and remove meat. Dip in lemon butter.

Tandoori-Spiced Salmon-and-Potatoes and Apple Cider Mussels

Prep time: 10 minutes | Cook time: 28 minutes Tandoori-Spiced Salmon and Potatoes | Serves 2:

455 g Fingerling or new potatoes	½ teaspoon smoked paprika
2 tablespoons vegetable oil, divided	¼ teaspoon cayenne pepper
	2 (170 g) skin-on salmon fillets
Kosher or coarse sea salt and freshly ground black pepper, to taste	Apple Cider Mussels| Serves 5:
	900 g mussels, cleaned and de-bearded
1 teaspoon ground turmeric	1 teaspoon onion powder
1 teaspoon ground cumin	1 teaspoon ground cumin
1 teaspoon ground ginger	1 tablespoon avocado oil
	60 ml apple cider vinegar

1. Preheat the air fryer to 180°C. 2. In a bowl, toss the potatoes with 1 tablespoon of the oil until evenly coated. Season with salt and pepper. Meanwhile, in a bowl, combine the remaining 1 tablespoon oil, the turmeric, cumin, ginger, paprika, and cayenne. Add the salmon fillets and turn in the spice mixture until fully coated all over. 3. Mix mussels with onion powder, ground cumin, avocado oil, and apple cider vinegar. Transfer the potatoes to the zone 1. Put the mussels in the zone 2. 4. Set the temperature 200°C. Set the time to 20 minutes for the zone 1 and 2 minutes for the zone 2. Set the AIR FRY. Select START. 5. After the potatoes have cooked for 20 minutes, place the salmon fillets, skin-side up, on top of the potatoes, and continue cooking until the potatoes are tender, the salmon is cooked, and the salmon skin is slightly crisp. 6. Transfer the salmon fillets to two plates and serve with the potatoes while both are warm.

Salmon Croquettes and Golden Beer-Battered Cod

Prep time: 15 minutes | Cook time: 15 minutes | Serves 4

Salmon Croquettes:	sauce
1 tablespoon vegetable oil	Golden Beer-Battered Cod:
75 g breadcrumbs	2 eggs
420 g can salmon, drained and all skin and fat removed	240 ml malty beer
	120 g plain flour
1 egg, beaten	60 g cornflour
25 g coarsely crushed salted crackers	1 teaspoon garlic powder
	Salt and pepper, to taste
½ teaspoon Old Bay Seasoning	4 cod fillets, 110 g each
½ teaspoon onion powder	Cooking spray
½ teaspoon Worcestershire	

1. Preheat the air fryer to 180°C. 2. In a shallow dish, mix oil and breadcrumbs until crumbly. 3. In a large bowl, combine the salmon, egg, cracker crumbs, Old Bay, onion powder, and Worcestershire. Mix well and shape into 8 small patties about ½-inch thick. 4. Gently dip each patty into bread crumb mixture and turn to coat well on all sides. Put them in the zone 1. 5. In a shallow bowl, beat together the eggs with the beer. In another shallow bowl, thoroughly combine the flour and cornflour. Sprinkle with the garlic powder, salt, and pepper. 6. Dredge each cod fillet in the flour mixture, then in the egg mixture. Dip each piece of fish in the flour mixture a second time. 7. Spritz the zone 2 with cooking spray. Arrange the cod fillets in the zone 2 in a single layer. 8. Set the temperature to 200°C. Set the time to 7 to 8 minutes for the zone 1 and 15 minutes for the zone 2, until outside is crispy and browned and the cod reaches an internal temperature of 64°C on a meat thermometer and the outside is crispy. Select AIR FRY. Select START. 9. Flip the fillets halfway through the cooking time. 10. Let the fish cool for 5 minutes and serve.

Country Prawns and Salmon Spring Rolls

Prep time: 30 minutes | Cook time: 15 minutes | Serves 4

455 g large prawns, peeled and deveined, with tails on	Salmon Spring Rolls:
	230 g salmon fillet
455 g smoked sausage, cut into thick slices	1 teaspoon toasted sesame oil
	1 onion, sliced
2 corn cobs, quartered	8 rice paper wrappers
1 courgette, cut into bite-sized pieces	1 yellow bell pepper, thinly sliced
1 red bell pepper, cut into chunks	1 carrot, shredded
	10 g chopped fresh flat-leaf parsley
1 tablespoon Old Bay seasoning	
2 tablespoons olive oil	15 g chopped fresh basil
Cooking spray	

1. Preheat the air fryer to 180°C. Spray the air fryer basket lightly with cooking spray. 2. In a large bowl, mix the prawns, sausage, corn, courgette, bell pepper, and Old Bay seasoning, and toss to coat with the spices. Add the olive oil and toss again until evenly coated. 3. Spread the mixture in the zone 1 in a single layer. You will need to cook in batches. Put the salmon in the zone 2 and drizzle with the sesame oil. Add the onion. 4. Set the temperature to 200°C for 15 to 20 minutes, or until cooked through, shaking the basket every 5 minutes for even cooking. Set the temperature to 190°C for 8 to 10 minutes, or until the salmon just flakes when tested with a fork and the onion is tender. Select AIR FRY. Select START. 5. Meanwhile, fill a small shallow bowl with warm water. One at a time, dip the rice paper wrappers into the water and place on a work surface. 6. Top each wrapper with one-eighth each of the salmon and onion mixture, yellow bell pepper, carrot, parsley, and basil. Roll up the wrapper, folding in the sides, to enclose the ingredients. 7. If you like, bake in the air fryer at 190°C for 7 to 9 minutes, until the rolls are crunchy. Cut the rolls in half to serve.

Lemony Prawns-and-Courgette and Sea Bass with Avocado Cream

Prep time: 45 minutes | Cook time: 9 minutes | Serves 4

Lemony Prawns and Courgette:
570 g extra-large raw prawns, peeled and deveined
2 medium courgettes (about 230 g each), halved lengthwise and cut into ½-inch-thick slices
1½ tablespoons olive oil
½ teaspoon garlic salt
1½ teaspoons dried oregano
⅛ teaspoon crushed red pepper flakes (optional)
Juice of ½ lemon
1 tablespoon chopped fresh mint
1 tablespoon chopped fresh dill
Sea Bass with Avocado Cream
Fish Fillets:
1½ tablespoons balsamic vinegar
120 ml vegetable broth
⅓ teaspoon shallot powder
1 tablespoon coconut aminos, or tamari
4 Sea Bass fillets
1 teaspoon ground black pepper
1½ tablespoons olive oil
Fine sea salt, to taste
⅓ teaspoon garlic powder
Avocado Cream:
2 tablespoons Greek-style yogurt
1 clove garlic, peeled and minced
1 teaspoon ground black pepper
½ tablespoon olive oil
80 ml vegetable broth
1 avocado
½ teaspoon lime juice
⅓ teaspoon fine sea salt

1. Preheat the air fryer to 180ºC. 2. In a large bowl, combine the prawns, courgette, oil, garlic salt, oregano, and pepper flakes (if using) and toss to coat. 3. Working in batches, arrange a single layer of the prawns and courgette in the zone 1. 4. In a bowl, wash and pat the fillets dry using some paper towels. Add all the seasonings. In another bowl, stir in the remaining ingredients for the fish fillets. 5. Add the seasoned fish fillets; cover and let the fillets marinate in your refrigerator at least 3 hours. 6. Set the temperature to 200ºC for 7 to 8 minutes for the zone 1. Set the temperature to 160ºC for 9 minutes for the zone 2. Select AIR FRY. Select START, shaking the basket halfway, until the courgette is golden and the prawns are cooked through. 6. Transfer to a serving dish and tent with foil while you air fry the remaining prawns and courgette. 7. Top with the lemon juice, mint, and dill and serve. 8. In the meantime, prepare the avocado sauce by mixing all the ingredients with an immersion blender or regular blender. Serve the sea bass fillets topped with the avocado sauce. Enjoy!

Cod with Jalapeño and Coconut Prawns with Spicy Dipping Sauce

Prep time: 20 minutes | Cook time: 14 minutes | Serves 4

Cod with Jalapeño:
4 cod fillets, boneless
1 jalapeño, minced
1 tablespoon avocado oil
½ teaspoon minced garlic
Coconut Prawns with Spicy Dipping Sauce:
70 g pork scratchings
70 g desiccated, unsweetened coconut
85 g coconut flour
1 teaspoon onion powder
1 teaspoon garlic powder
2 eggs
680 g large prawns, peeled and deveined
½ teaspoon salt
¼ teaspoon freshly ground black pepper
Spicy Dipping Sauce:
115 g mayonnaise
2 tablespoons Sriracha
Zest and juice of ½ lime
1 clove garlic, minced

1. Preheat the air fryer to 180ºC. In the shallow bowl, mix minced jalapeño, avocado oil, and minced garlic. 2. In another shallow bowl, combine the coconut flour, onion powder, and garlic powder; mix until thoroughly combined. 3. In a third shallow bowl, whisk the eggs until slightly frothy. 4. In a large bowl, season the prawns with the salt and pepper, tossing gently to coat. 5 Put the cod fillets in the zone 1 in one layer and top with minced jalapeño mixture. 6. In a food processor fitted with a metal blade, combine the pork scratchings and desiccated coconut. Pulse until the mixture resembles coarse crumbs. Transfer to a shallow bowl. 7. Working a few pieces at a time, dredge the prawns in the flour mixture, followed by the eggs, and finishing with the pork rind crumb mixture. Arrange the prawns on a baking sheet until ready to air fry. 8. Working in batches if necessary, arrange the prawns in a single layer in the zone 2. 9. Set the temperature to 190ºC for 7 minutes per side for the zone 1. Set the temperature 200ºC for 8 minutes for the zone 2. Select AIR FRY. Select START. Pausing halfway through the cooking time to turn the prawns, until cooked through. 10. To make the sauce: In a small bowl, combine the mayonnaise, Sriracha, lime zest and juice, and garlic. Whisk until thoroughly combined. Serve alongside the prawns.

Chapter 7 Snacks and Appetizers

Chapter 7 Snacks and Appetizer

Cheese Drops and Polenta Fries with Chilli-Lime Mayo

Prep time: 25 minutes | Cook time: 28 minutes per batch

Cheese Drops | Serves 8:
177 ml plain flour
½ teaspoon rock salt
¼ teaspoon cayenne pepper
¼ teaspoon smoked paprika
¼ teaspoon black pepper
Dash garlic powder (optional)
60 ml butter, softened
240 ml shredded extra mature Cheddar cheese, at room temperature
Olive oil spray
Polenta Fries with Chilli-Lime Mayo:
Polenta Fries:
2 teaspoons vegetable or olive oil
¼ teaspoon paprika
450 g prepared polenta, cut into 3-inch × ½-inch strips
Chilli-Lime Mayo:
120 ml mayonnaise
1 teaspoon chilli powder
1 teaspoon chopped fresh coriander
¼ teaspoon ground cumin
Juice of ½ lime
Salt and freshly ground black pepper, to taste

1. Preheat the air fryer to 180°C. In a small bowl, combine the flour, salt, cayenne, paprika, pepper, and garlic powder, if using. 2. Using a food processor, cream the butter and cheese until smooth. Gently add the seasoned flour and process until the dough is well combined, smooth, and no longer sticky. (Or make the dough in a stand mixer fitted with the paddle attachment: Cream the butter and cheese on medium speed until smooth, then add the seasoned flour and beat at low speed until smooth.) 3. Divide the dough into 32 equal-size pieces. On a lightly floured surface, roll each piece into a small ball. 4. Spray the zone 1 with oil spray. Arrange 16 cheese drops in the zone 1. 5. Mix the oil and paprika in a bowl. Add the polenta strips and toss until evenly coated. Transfer the polenta strips to the zone 2. 6. Set the temperature to 160°C for 10 minutes for the zone 1, or until drops are just starting to brown. Set the temperature to 200°C for 28 minutes for the zone 2 until the fries are golden brown. Select AIR FRY. Select START, shaking the basket once during cooking. Season as desired with salt and pepper in the zone 2. Transfer to a wire rack. Repeat with remaining dough, checking for doneness at 8 minutes. 7. Cool the cheese drops completely on the wire rack. Store in an airtight container until ready to serve, or up to 1 or 2 days. 8. Meanwhile, whisk together all the ingredients for the chilli-lime mayo in a small bowl. 9. Remove the polenta fries from the air fryer to a plate and serve alongside the chilli-lime mayo as a dipping sauce.

Cheesy Steak Fries and Baked Spanakopita Dip

Prep time: 15 minutes | Cook time: 20 minutes

Cheesy Steak Fries | Serves 5:
1 (794 g) bag frozen steak fries
Cooking spray
Salt and pepper, to taste
120 ml beef gravy
240 ml shredded Mozzarella cheese
2 spring onions, green parts only, chopped
with gravy and sprinkle the spring onions on top for a green garnish. Serve.
Baked Spanakopita Dip | Serves 2
Olive oil cooking spray
3 tablespoons olive oil, divided
2 tablespoons minced white onion
2 garlic cloves, minced
1 L fresh spinach
113 g soft white cheese, softened
113 g feta cheese, divided
Zest of 1 lemon
¼ teaspoon ground nutmeg
1 teaspoon dried dill
½ teaspoon salt
Pitta chips, carrot sticks, or sliced bread for serving (optional)

1. Preheat the air fryer to 180°C. 2. Coat the inside of a 6-inch ramekin or baking dish with olive oil cooking spray. 3. In a large skillet over medium heat, heat 1 tablespoon of the olive oil. Add the onion, then cook for 1 minute. 4. Add in the garlic and cook, stirring for 1 minute more. 5. Reduce the heat to low and mix in the spinach and water. 6. Place the frozen steak fries in the zone 1. Set the temperature to 200°C. Set the time to 10 minutes for the zone 1 and 2 to 3 minutes for the zone 2. Select AIR FRY. Select START. Shake the basket and spritz the fries with cooking spray. Sprinkle with salt and pepper. Air fry for an additional 8 minutes, or until the spinach has wilted. Remove the skillet from the heat. 6. In a medium bowl, combine the soft white cheese, 57 g of the feta, and the remaining 2 tablespoons of olive oil, along with the lemon zest, nutmeg, dill, and salt. Mix until just combined. 7. Add the vegetables to the cheese base and stir until combined. 8. Pour the dip mixture into the prepared ramekin and top with the remaining 57 g of feta cheese. 9. Pour the beef gravy into a medium, microwave-safe bowl. Microwave for 30 seconds, or until the gravy is warm. 10. Sprinkle the fries with the cheese. Air fry for an additional 2 minutes, until the cheese is melted. 11. Transfer the fries to a serving dish. Drizzle the fries. 12. Serve with pitta chips, carrot sticks, or sliced bread.

Italian Rice Balls

Prep time: 20 minutes | Cook time: 10 minutes | Makes 8 rice balls

355 ml cooked sticky rice
½ teaspoon Italian seasoning blend
¾ teaspoon salt, divided
8 black olives, pitted
28 g Mozzarella cheese, cut into tiny pieces (small enough to stuff into olives)
2 eggs
80 ml Italian breadcrumbs
177 ml panko breadcrumbs
Cooking spray

1. Preheat air fryer to 180°C. 2. Stuff each black olive with a piece of Mozzarella cheese. Set aside. 3. In a bowl, combine the cooked sticky rice, Italian seasoning blend, and ½ teaspoon of salt and stir to mix well. Form the rice mixture into a log with your hands and divide it into 8 equal portions. Mould each portion around a black olive and roll into a ball. 4. Transfer to the freezer to chill for 10 to 15 minutes until firm. 5. In a shallow dish, place the Italian breadcrumbs. In a separate shallow dish, whisk the eggs. In a third shallow dish, combine the panko breadcrumbs and remaining salt. 6. One by one, roll the rice balls in the Italian breadcrumbs, then dip in the whisked eggs, finally coat them with the panko breadcrumbs. 7. Arrange the rice balls in the dual zone air fryer and spritz both sides with cooking spray. 8. Air fry for 10 minutes until the rice balls are golden brown. Flip the balls halfway through the cooking time. 9. Serve warm.

Authentic Scotch Eggs

Prep time: 15 minutes | Cook time: 11 to 13 minutes | Serves 6

680 g bulk lean chicken or turkey sausage
3 raw eggs, divided
355 ml dried breadcrumbs, divided
120 ml plain flour
6 hardboiled eggs, peeled
Cooking oil spray

1. In a large bowl, combine the chicken sausage, 1 raw egg, and 120 ml of breadcrumbs and mix well. Divide the mixture into 6 pieces and flatten each into a long oval. 2. In a shallow bowl, beat the remaining 2 raw eggs. 3. Place the flour in a small bowl. 4. Place the remaining 240 ml of breadcrumbs in a second small bowl. 5. Roll each hardboiled egg in the flour and wrap one of the chicken sausage pieces around each egg to encircle it completely. 6. One at a time, roll the encased eggs in the flour, dip in the beaten eggs, and finally dip in the breadcrumbs to coat. 7. Insert the crisper plate into the basket and the basket into the unit. Preheat the unit by selecting AIR FRY, setting the temperature to 192°C, and setting the time to 3 minutes. Select START to begin. 8. Once the unit is preheated, spray the crisper plate with cooking oil. Place the eggs in a single layer into the dual zone and spray them with oil. 9. Select AIR FRY, set the temperature to 192°C, and set the time to 13 minutes. Select START to begin. 10. After about 6 minutes, use tongs to turn the eggs and spray them with more oil. Resume cooking for 5 to 7 minutes more, or until the chicken is thoroughly cooked and the Scotch eggs are browned. 11. When the cooking is complete, serve warm.

Taco-Spiced Chickpeas and Greek Potato Skins with Olives-and-Feta

Prep time: 10 minutes | Cook time: 45 minutes | Serves 3

Taco-Spiced Chickpeas:
Oil, for spraying
1 (439 g) can chickpeas, drained
1 teaspoon chilli powder
½ teaspoon ground cumin
½ teaspoon salt
½ teaspoon granulated garlic
2 teaspoons lime juice
Greek Potato Skins with Olives-and-Feta | Serves 4:
2 russet or Maris Piper potatoes
3 tablespoons olive oil, divided, plus more for drizzling (optional)
1 teaspoon rock salt, divided
¼ teaspoon black pepper
2 tablespoons fresh coriander, chopped, plus more for serving
60 ml Kalamata olives, diced
60 ml crumbled feta
Chopped fresh parsley, for garnish (optional)

1. Preheat the air fryer to 180°C. Line the zone 1 with parchment and spray lightly with oil. Place the chickpeas in the zone 1. 2. Using a fork, poke 2 to 3 holes in the potatoes, then coat each with about ½ tablespoon olive oil and ½ teaspoon salt. Place the potatoes into the zone 2. 3. Set the temperature to 200°C. Set the time to 17 minutes and slect AIR FRY for the zone 1, shaking or stirring the chickpeas and spraying lightly with oil every 5 to 7 minutes. Set the time to 30 minutes and select BAKE for the zone 2. Select START. 4. In a small bowl, mix together the chilli powder, cumin, salt, and garlic. 5. When 2 to 3 minutes of cooking time remain, sprinkle half of the seasoning mix over the chickpeas. Finish cooking. 6. Transfer the chickpeas to a medium bowl and toss with the remaining seasoning mix and the lime juice. Serve immediately. 7. Remove the potatoes from the zone 2, and slice in half. Using a spoon, scoop out the flesh of the potatoes, leaving a ½-inch layer of potato inside the skins, and set the skins aside. 10. In a medium bowl, combine the scooped potato middles with the remaining 2 tablespoons of olive oil, ½ teaspoon of salt, black pepper, and coriander. Mix until well combined. 8. Divide the potato filling into the now-empty potato skins, spreading it evenly over them. Top each potato with a tablespoon each of the olives and feta. 9. Place the loaded potato skins back into the zone 2 and bake for 15 minutes. 10. Serve with additional chopped coriander or parsley and a drizzle of olive oil, if desired.

Jalapeño Poppers and Greens Chips with Curried Yoghurt Sauce

Prep time: 20 minutes | Cook time: 20 minutes | Serves 4

Jalapeño Poppers:
Oil, for spraying
227 g soft white cheese
177 ml gluten-free breadcrumbs, divided
2 tablespoons chopped fresh parsley
½ teaspoon granulated garlic
½ teaspoon salt
10 jalapeño peppers, halved and seeded
Greens Chips with Curried Yoghurt Sauce:
240 ml low-fat Greek yoghurt
1 tablespoon freshly squeezed lemon juice
1 tablespoon curry powder
½ bunch curly kale, stemmed, ribs removed and discarded, leaves cut into 2- to 3-inch pieces
½ bunch chard, stemmed, ribs removed and discarded, leaves cut into 2- to 3-inch pieces
1½ teaspoons olive oil

1. Line the zone 1 with parchment and spray lightly with oil. 2. In a medium bowl, mix together the soft white cheese, half of the breadcrumbs, the parsley, garlic, and salt. 3. Spoon the mixture into the jalapeño halves. Gently press the stuffed jalapeños in the remaining breadcrumbs. 4. In a small bowl, stir together the yoghurt, lemon juice, and curry powder. Set aside. 5. In a large bowl, toss the kale and chard with the olive oil, working the oil into the leaves with your hands. This helps break up the fibres in the leaves so the chips are tender. 6. Place the stuffed jalapeños in the prepared zone 1. 6. Set the temperature to 190°C for 20 minutes for the zone 1, or until the cheese is melted and the breadcrumbs are crisp and golden brown. Set the temperature to 200°C for 5 to 6 minutes for the zone 2, or until crisp, shaking the basket once during cooking. Select AIR FRY. Select SATRT. Serve with the yoghurt sauce.

Kale Chips with Sesame and Root Veggie Chips with Herb Salt

Prep time: 25 minutes | Cook time: 8 minutes | Serves 5

Kale Chips with Sesame:
2 L deribbed kale leaves, torn into 2-inch pieces
1½ tablespoons olive oil
¾ teaspoon chilli powder
¼ teaspoon garlic powder
½ teaspoon paprika
2 teaspoons sesame seeds
Root Veggie Chips with Herb Salt | Serves 2:
1 parsnip, washed
1 small beetroot, washed
1 small turnip, washed
½ small sweet potato, washed
1 teaspoon olive oil
Cooking spray
Herb Salt:
¼ teaspoon rock salt
2 teaspoons finely chopped fresh parsley

1. Preheat air fryer to 180°C. 2. In a large bowl, toss the kale with the olive oil, chilli powder, garlic powder, paprika, and sesame seeds until well coated. 3. Peel and thinly slice the parsnip, beetroot, turnip, and sweet potato, then place the vegetables in a large bowl, add the olive oil, and toss. Put the kale in the zone 1. Spray the zone 2 with cooking spray, then place the vegetables in the zone 2. 4. Set the temperature to 200°C. Set the time to 8 minutes. Select AIR FRY. Select START, flipping the kale twice during cooking, or until the kale is crispy, gently shaking the basket halfway through. 5. While the chips cook, make the herb salt in a small bowl by combining the rock salt and parsley. 6. Remove the chips and place on a serving plate, then sprinkle the herb salt on top and allow to cool for 2 to 3 minutes before serving. Serve warm.

Goat Cheese-and-Garlic Crostini and Garlic-Roasted Tomatoes and Olives

Prep time: 8 minutes | Cook time: 20 minutes

Goat Cheese and Garlic Crostini | Serves 4
1 wholemeal baguette
60 ml olive oil
2 garlic cloves, minced
113 g goat cheese
2 tablespoons fresh basil, minced
Garlic-Roasted Tomatoes and Olives | Serves 6:
475 ml cherry tomatoes
4 garlic cloves, roughly chopped
½ red onion, roughly chopped
240 ml black olives
240 ml green olives
1 tablespoon fresh basil, minced
1 tablespoon fresh oregano, minced
2 tablespoons olive oil
¼ to ½ teaspoon salt

1. Preheat the air fryer to 180°C. 2. Cut the baguette into ½-inch-thick slices. 3. In a small bowl, mix together the olive oil and garlic, then brush it over one side of each slice of bread. 4. Place the olive-oil-coated bread in a single layer in the zone 1. 5. In a large bowl, combine all of the ingredients and toss together so that the tomatoes and olives are coated well with the olive oil and herbs. 6. Pour the mixture into the zone 2. 7. Set the temperature to 200°C. Set the time to 5 minutes and select BAKE for the zone 1. Set the 10 minutes and select ROAST for the zone 2. Select AIR FRY. Select START. Stir the mixture well, then continue roasting for an additional 10 minutes. 8. Meanwhile, in a small bowl, mix together the goat cheese and basil. 9. Remove the toast from the air fryer, then spread a thin layer of the goat cheese mixture over the top of each piece and serve. 10. Remove from the air fryer, transfer to a serving bowl, and enjoy.
e serving with vegetables, toasted baguette slices, pitta chips, or tortilla chips.

Rumaki and Cheese-Stuffed Blooming Onion

Prep time: 40 minutes | Cook time: 15 minutes per batch

Rumaki | Serves 24
283 g raw chicken livers
1 can sliced water chestnuts, drained
60 ml low-salt teriyaki sauce
12 slices turkey bacon
Cheese-Stuffed Blooming Onion| Serves 2:
1 large brown onion (397 g)
1 tablespoon olive oil
Rock salt and freshly ground black pepper, to taste
60 ml plus 2 tablespoons panko breadcrumbs
60 ml grated Parmesan cheese
3 tablespoons mayonnaise
1 tablespoon fresh lemon juice
1 tablespoon chopped fresh flat-leaf parsley
2 teaspoons whole-grain Dijon mustard
1 garlic clove, minced

1. Cut livers into 1½-inch pieces, trimming out tough veins as you slice. 2. Place livers, water chestnuts, and teriyaki sauce in small container with lid. If needed, add another tablespoon of teriyaki sauce to make sure livers are covered. Refrigerate for 1 hour. 3. When ready to cook, cut bacon slices in half crosswise. 4. Wrap 1 piece of liver and 1 slice of water chestnut in each bacon strip. Secure with toothpick. 5. When you have wrapped half of the livers, place them in the zone 1 in a single layer. 6. Place the onion on a cutting board and trim the top off and peel off the outer skin. Turn the onion upside down and use a paring knife, cut vertical slits halfway through the onion at ½-inch intervals around the onion, keeping the root intact. When you turn the onion right side up, it should open up like the petals of a flower. Drizzle the cut sides of the onion with the olive oil and season with salt and pepper. Place petal-side up in the zone 2. 7. Set the temperature to 200ºC for 10 to 12 minutes for the zone 1 until liver is done, and bacon is crispy. Set the temperaturre to 180ºC for 10 minutes for the zone 2. Select AIR FRY. Select START. 7. While first batch cooks, wrap the remaining livers. Repeat step 6 to cook your second batch. 8. Meanwhile, in a bowl, stir together the panko, Parmesan, mayonnaise, lemon juice, parsley, mustard, and garlic until incorporated into a smooth paste. 9. Remove the onion from the fryer and stuff the paste all over and in between the onion "petals." Return the onion to the air fryer and air fry at 190ºC until the onion is tender in the centre and the bread crumb mixture is golden brown, about 5 minutes. Remove the onion from the air fryer, transfer to a plate, and serve hot.

Peppery Chicken Meatballs and Pepperoni Pizza Dip

Prep time: 15 minutes | Cook time: 13 minutes

Peppery Chicken Meatballs | Serves 16
2 teaspoons olive oil
60 ml minced onion
60 ml minced red pepper
2 vanilla wafers, crushed
1 egg white
½ teaspoon dried thyme
230 g minced chicken breast
Pepperoni Pizza Dip | Serves 6:
170 g soft white cheese
177 ml shredded Italian cheese blend
60 ml sour cream
1½ teaspoons dried Italian seasoning
¼ teaspoon garlic salt
¼ teaspoon onion powder
177 ml pizza sauce
120 ml sliced miniature pepperoni
60 ml sliced black olives
1 tablespoon thinly sliced green onion
Cut-up raw vegetables, toasted baguette slices, pitta chips, or tortilla chips, for serving

1.Preheat the air fryer to 180ºC. 2. In a baking pan, mix the olive oil, onion, and red pepper. Put the pan in the zone 1. 3. In a small bowl, combine the soft white cheese, 60 ml of the shredded cheese, the sour cream, Italian seasoning, garlic salt, and onion powder. Stir until smooth and the ingredients are well blended. 4. Spread the mixture in the dual zone baking pan. Top with the pizza sauce, spreading to the edges. Sprinkle with the remaining 120 ml shredded cheese. Arrange the pepperoni slices on top of the cheese. Top with the black olives and green onion. Place the pan in the zone 2. 5. Set the temperature to 200ºC. Set the time to 3 to 5 minutes for the zone 1, or until the vegetables are tender. Set the time to 10 minutes for the zone 2, or until the pepperoni is beginning to brown on the edges and the cheese is bubbly and lightly browned. Select AIR FRY. Select START. 6. In a medium bowl, mix the cooked vegetables, crushed wafers, egg white, and thyme until well combined. 7. Mix in the chicken, gently but thoroughly, until everything is combined. 8. Form the mixture into 16 meatballs and place them in the zone 1. Air fry for 10 to 15 minutes, or until the meatballs reach an internal temperature of 74ºC on a meat thermometer. Serve immediately.

Garlicky-and-Cheesy French Fries and Crunchy Basil White Beans

Prep time: 7 minutes | Cook time: 20 minutes

Garlicky and Cheesy French Fries | Serves 4:
3 medium russet or Maris Piper potatoes, rinsed, dried, and cut into thin wedges or classic fry shapes
2 tablespoons extra-virgin olive oil
1 tablespoon granulated garlic
80 ml grated Parmesan cheese
½ teaspoon salt
¼ teaspoon freshly ground black pepper
Cooking oil spray
2 tablespoons finely chopped fresh parsley (optional)

Crunchy Basil White Beans | Serves 2:
1 (425 g) can cooked white beans
2 tablespoons olive oil
1 teaspoon fresh sage, chopped
¼ teaspoon garlic powder
¼ teaspoon salt, divided
1 teaspoon chopped fresh basil

1. Preheat the air fryer to 180°C. In a large bowl combine the potato wedges or fries and the olive oil. Toss to coat. 2. Sprinkle the potatoes with the granulated garlic, Parmesan cheese, salt, and pepper, and toss again. 3. Insert the crisper plate into the basket and the basket into the unit. 4. Once the unit is preheated, spray the crisper plate with cooking oil. 5. In a medium bowl, mix together the beans, olive oil, sage, garlic, ⅛ teaspoon salt, and basil. 6. Place the potatoes into the zone 1. Pour the white beans into the zone 2 and spread them out in a single layer. 7. Set the temperature to 200°C. Set the time to 20 to 25 minutes and select AIR FRY for the zone 1. Set the time to 10 minutes and select BAKE for the zone 2. Select START to begin. Stir and continue cooking for an additional 5 to 9 minutes, or until they reach your preferred level of crispiness. 8. After about 10 minutes, remove the basket and shake it so the fries at the bottom come up to the top. Reinsert the basket to resume cooking. 9. Toss with the remaining ⅛ teaspoon salt before serving. 10. When the cooking is complete, top the fries with the parsley (if using) and serve hot.

Chapter 8 Vegetables and Sides

Chapter 8 Vegetables and Sides

Breaded Green Tomatoes and Garlic Cauliflower with Tahini

Prep time: 25 minutes | Cook time: 30 minutes | Serves 4

Breaded Green Tomatoes:
60 g plain flour
2 eggs
60 g semolina
60 g panko bread crumbs
1 teaspoon garlic powder
Salt and freshly ground black pepper, to taste
2 green tomatoes, cut into ½-inch-thick rounds
Cooking oil spray
Garlic Cauliflower with Tahini:
Cauliflower:
500 g cauliflower florets (about 1 large head)
6 garlic cloves, smashed and cut into thirds
3 tablespoons vegetable oil
½ teaspoon ground cumin
½ teaspoon ground coriander
½ teaspoon coarse sea salt
Sauce:
2 tablespoons tahini (sesame paste)
2 tablespoons hot water
1 tablespoon fresh lemon juice
1 teaspoon minced garlic
½ teaspoon coarse sea salt

1. Preheat the unit by selecting AIR FRY, setting the temperature to 200°C, and setting the time to 3 minutes. Select START to begin. Place the flour in a small bowl. 2. In another small bowl, beat the eggs. 3. In a third small bowl, stir together the semolina, panko, and garlic powder. Season with salt and pepper. 4. Dip each tomato slice into the flour, the egg, and finally the semolina mixture to coat. 5. Insert the crisper plate into the zone 1. 6. For the cauliflower: In a large bowl, combine the cauliflower florets and garlic. Drizzle with the vegetable oil. Sprinkle with the cumin, coriander, and salt. Toss until well coated. 7. Once the unit is preheated, spray the crisper plate and the basket with cooking oil. Working in batches, place the tomato slices in the zone 1 in a single layer. Do not stack them. Spray the tomato slices with the cooking oil. Place the cauliflower in the zone 2. 8. Set the temperature to 200°C. Set the time to 10 minutes for the zone 1 and 20 minutes for the zone 2. Select AIR FRY. Select START to begin, turning the cauliflower halfway through the cooking time. 9. After 5 minutes, use tongs to flip the tomatoes. Resume cooking for 4 to 5 minutes, or until crisp. 10. When the cooking is complete, transfer the fried green tomatoes to a plate. Repeat steps 6, 7, and 8 for the remaining tomatoes. 11. Meanwhile, for the sauce: In a small bowl, combine the tahini, water, lemon juice, garlic, and salt. (The sauce will appear curdled at first, but keep stirring until you have a thick, creamy, smooth mixture.) 12. Transfer the cauliflower to a large serving bowl. Pour the sauce over and toss gently to coat. Serve immediately.

Broccoli with Sesame Dressing and Courgette Fritters

Prep time: 15 minutes | Cook time: 10 minutes | Serves 4

Broccoli with Sesame Dressing:
425 g broccoli florets, cut into bite-size pieces
1 tablespoon olive oil
¼ teaspoon salt
2 tablespoons sesame seeds
2 tablespoons rice vinegar
2 tablespoons coconut aminos
2 tablespoons sesame oil
½ teaspoon xylitol
¼ teaspoon red pepper flakes (optional)
Make the Courgette Fritters:
2 courgette, grated (about 450 g)
1 teaspoon salt
25 g almond flour
20 g grated Parmesan cheese
1 large egg
¼ teaspoon dried thyme
¼ teaspoon ground turmeric
¼ teaspoon freshly ground black pepper
1 tablespoon olive oil
½ lemon, sliced into wedges

1. Preheat the air fryer to 180°C. 2. In a large bowl, toss the broccoli with the olive oil and salt until thoroughly coated. 3. Transfer the broccoli to the zone 1. Pausing halfway through the cooking time to shake the basket. 3. Cut a piece of parchment paper to fit slightly smaller than the bottom of the zone 2. 4. Place the courgette in a large colander and sprinkle with the salt. Let sit for 5 to 10 minutes. Squeeze as much liquid as you can from the courgette and place in a large mixing bowl. Add the almond flour, Parmesan, egg, thyme, turmeric, and black pepper. Stir gently until thoroughly combined. 5. Shape the mixture into 8 patties and arrange on the parchment paper. Brush lightly with the olive oil. 6. Set the temperature to 180°C. Set the time to 10 minutes. Select AIR FRY. Select MATCH COOK. Select START. Until golden brown and the stems are tender and the edges are beginning to crisp. 7. Meanwhile, in the same large bowl, whisk together the sesame seeds, vinegar, coconut aminos, sesame oil, xylitol, and red pepper flakes (if using). 8. Transfer the broccoli to the bowl and toss until thoroughly coated with the seasonings. Pausing halfway through the cooking time to turn the patties. Serve warm with the lemon wedges.

Courgette Balls-and-Bacon Potatoes and Green Beans

Prep time: 15 minutes | Cook time: 25 minutes | Serves 4

Courgette Balls and Bacon Potatoes:	Oil, for spraying
4 courgettes	900 g medium Maris Piper potatoes, quartered
1 egg	100 g bacon bits
45 g grated Parmesan cheese	280 g fresh green beans
1 tablespoon Italian herbs	1 teaspoon salt
75 g grated coconut	½ teaspoon freshly ground black pepper
Green Beans:	

1. Preheat the air fryer to 180ºC. Thinly grate the courgettes and dry with a cheesecloth, ensuring to remove all the moisture. 2. In a bowl, combine the courgettes with the egg, Parmesan, Italian herbs, and grated coconut, mixing well to incorporate everything. Using the hands, mold the mixture into balls. 3. Lay the courgette balls in the zone 1. Line the zone 2 with parchment and spray lightly with oil. 4. Place the potatoes in the zone 2. Top with the bacon bits and green beans. Sprinkle with the salt and black pepper and spray liberally with oil. 5. Set the temperatue to 200ºC for 10 minutes for the zone 1. Set the temperature to 180ºC for 25 minutes for the zone 2. Select AIR FRY. Select START, stirring after 12 minutes and spraying with oil, until the potatoes are easily pierced with a fork. Serve hot.

Mashed Sweet Potato Tots and Parsnip Fries with Romesco Sauce

Prep time: 30 minutes | Cook time: 24 minutes per batch Mashed Sweet Potato Tots | Serves 18 to 24:

210 g cooked mashed sweet potatoes	Olive oil
1 egg white, beaten	½ Jalapeño pepper, seeded
⅛ teaspoon ground cinnamon	1 tablespoon fresh parsley leaves
1 dash nutmeg	1 clove garlic
2 tablespoons chopped pecans	2 plum tomatoes, peeled and seeded
1½ teaspoons honey	1 tablespoon red wine vinegar
Salt, to taste	¼ teaspoon smoked paprika
50 g panko bread crumbs	½ teaspoon salt
Oil for misting or cooking spray	180 ml olive oil
Parsnip Fries with Romesco Sauce	Serves 4:	3 parsnips, peeled and cut into long strips
Romesco Sauce:	2 teaspoons olive oil
1 red pepper, halved and seeded	Salt and freshly ground black pepper, to taste
1 (1-inch) thick slice of Italian bread, torn into pieces	
130 g almonds, toasted	

1. Preheat the air fryer to 180ºC. 2. In a large bowl, mix together the potatoes, egg white, cinnamon, nutmeg, pecans, honey, and salt to taste. 3. Place panko crumbs on a sheet of wax paper. 4. For each tot, use about 2 teaspoons of sweet potato mixture. To shape, drop the measure of potato mixture onto panko crumbs and push crumbs up and around potatoes to coat edges. Then turn tot over to coat other side with crumbs. 5. Place the red pepper halves, cut side down, in the zone 1. 6. Toss the torn bread and almonds with a little olive oil. 7. Mist tots with oil or cooking spray and place in zone 1 in single layer. 8. Combine the toasted bread, almonds, roasted red pepper, Jalapeño pepper, parsley, garlic, tomatoes, vinegar, smoked paprika and salt in a food processor or blender. Process until smooth. With the processor running, add the olive oil through the feed tube until the sauce comes together in a smooth paste that is barely pourable. 11. Toss the parsnip strips with the olive oil, salt and freshly ground black peppert in the zone 2. 9. Set the temperature to 200ºC. Set the time to 4 minutes for the zone 1 and 8 to 10 minutes for the zone 2 until browned and crispy and the skin turns black all over. Select AIR FRY. Select START. Remove the pepper from the air fryer and let it cool. 10. When it is cool enough to handle, peel the pepper, and shaking the basket a couple times throughout the cooking time. 11. When the bread and almonds are nicely toasted, remove them from the air fryer and let them cool for just a minute or two, shaking the basket a couple times during the cooking process so they brown and cook evenly. 12. Serve the parsnip fries warm with the Romesco sauce to dip into.

Rosemary-Roasted Red Potatoes and Crispy Green Beans

Prep time: 10 minutes | Cook time: 20 minutes | Serves 6

Rosemary-Roasted Red Potatoes:	Crispy Green Beans	Serves 4:
450 g red potatoes, quartered	2 teaspoons olive oil
65 ml olive oil	230 g fresh green beans, ends trimmed
½ teaspoon coarse sea salt	¼ teaspoon salt
¼ teaspoon black pepper	¼ teaspoon ground black pepper
1 garlic clove, minced	
4 rosemary sprigs	

1. Preheat the air fryer to 180ºC. 2. In a large bowl, toss the potatoes with the olive oil, salt, pepper, and garlic until well coated. 3. Pour the potatoes into the zone 1 and top with the sprigs of rosemary. 6. In a large bowl, drizzle olive oil over green beans and sprinkle with salt and pepper. Place green beans into ungreased in the zone 2. 4. Set the temperature to 200ºC and the time to 10 minutes for the zone 1. Set the temperature to 180ºC and the time to 8 minutes for the zone 2. Select ROAST for the zone 1 and AIR FRY for the zone 2. Select START, shaking the basket two times during cooking.then stir or toss the potatoes and roast for 10 minutes more. 5. Remove the rosemary sprigs and serve the potatoes. Season with additional salt and pepper, if needed. Green beans will be dark golden and crispy at the edges when done. Serve warm.

Dijon Roast Cabbage and Scalloped Potatoes

Prep time: 15 minutes | Cook time: 20 minutes | Serves 4

Dijon Roast Cabbage:
1 small head cabbage, cored and sliced into 1-inch-thick slices
2 tablespoons olive oil, divided
½ teaspoon salt
1 tablespoon Dijon mustard
1 teaspoon apple cider vinegar
1 teaspoon granular erythritol

Scalloped Potatoes:
440 g sliced frozen potatoes, thawed
3 cloves garlic, minced
Pinch salt
Freshly ground black pepper, to taste
180 g double cream

1. Preheat the air fryer to 180°C. Drizzle each cabbage slice with 1 tablespoon olive oil, then sprinkle with salt. 2. Toss the potatoes with the garlic, salt, and black pepper in a baking pan until evenly coated. Pour the double cream over the top. 3. Place slices into ungreased zone 1, working in batches if needed. Place the baking pan in the zone 2. 4. Set the temperature to 180°C. Set the time to 10 minutes and select AIR FRY for the zone 1. Set the time to 15 minutes and select BAKE for the zone 2, or until the potatoes are tender and top is golden brown. Select START. Cabbage will be tender and edges will begin to brown when done. 5. Check for doneness and bake for another 5 minutes as needed. 6. In a small bowl, whisk remaining olive oil with mustard, vinegar, and erythritol. Drizzle over cabbage in a large serving dish. Serve hot.

Citrus Sweet Potatoes and Carrots and Fried Courgette Salad

Prep time: 15 minutes | Cook time: 20 minutes | Serves 4

Citrus Sweet Potatoes and Carrots:
2 large carrots, cut into 1-inch chunks
1 medium sweet potato, peeled and cut into 1-inch cubes
25 g chopped onion
2 garlic cloves, minced
2 tablespoons honey
1 tablespoon freshly squeezed orange juice
2 teaspoons butter, melted

Fried Courgette Salad:
2 medium courgette, thinly sliced
5 tablespoons olive oil, divided
15 g chopped fresh parsley
2 tablespoons chopped fresh mint
Zest and juice of ½ lemon
1 clove garlic, minced
65 g crumbled feta cheese
Freshly ground black pepper, to taste

1. Insert the crisper plate into the basket and the basket into the unit. Preheat the unit by selecting AIR ROAST, setting the temperature to 180°C, and setting the time to 3 minutes. Select START to begin. 2. In a 6-by-2-inch round pan, toss together the carrots, sweet potato, onion, garlic, honey, orange juice, and melted butter to coat. 3. Once the unit is preheated, place the pan into zone 1. 4. In a large bowl, toss the courgette slices with 1 tablespoon of the olive oil. 5. Working in batches if necessary, arrange the courgette slices in an even layer in the zone 2. Pausing halfway through the cooking time to shake the basket. 6. Set the temperature to 200°C, and set the time to 25 minutes and select AIR ROAST for the zone 1. Set the time to 5 to 7 minutes and select AIR RY for the zone 2 until soft and lightly browned on each side. Select START to begin. 7. After 15 minutes, remove the zone 1 and shake the vegetables. Reinsert the basket to resume cooking. After 5 minutes, if the vegetables are tender and glazed, they are done. If not, resume cooking. 8. When the cooking is complete, serve immediately. 9. Meanwhile, in a small bowl, combine the remaining 4 tablespoons olive oil, parsley, mint, lemon zest, lemon juice, and garlic. 10. Arrange the courgette on a plate and drizzle with the dressing. Sprinkle the feta and black pepper on top. Serve warm or at room temperature.

Golden Pickles and Balsamic Brussels Sprouts

Prep time: 15 minutes | Cook time: 15 minutes | Serves 4

Golden Pickles:
14 dill pickles, sliced
30 g flour
⅛ teaspoon baking powder
Pinch of salt
2 tablespoons cornflour plus 3 tablespoons water
6 tablespoons panko bread crumbs
½ teaspoon paprika
Cooking spray

Balsamic Brussels Sprouts:
180 g trimmed and halved fresh Brussels sprouts
2 tablespoons olive oil
¼ teaspoon salt
¼ teaspoon ground black pepper
2 tablespoons balsamic vinegar
2 slices cooked sugar-free bacon, crumbled

1. Preheat the air fryer to 180°C. 2. Drain any excess moisture out of the dill pickles on a paper towel. 3. In a bowl, combine the flour, baking powder and salt. 4. Throw in the cornflour and water mixture and combine well with a whisk. 5. Put the panko bread crumbs in a shallow dish along with the paprika. Mix thoroughly. 6. Dip the pickles in the flour batter, before coating in the bread crumbs. Spritz all the pickles with the cooking spray. 7. Transfer to the zone 1. 8. In a large bowl, toss Brussels sprouts in olive oil, then sprinkle with salt and pepper. Place into ungreased zone 2. 9. Set the temperature to 190°C and the time to 15 minutes for the zone 1, or until golden brown. Set the temperature to 190°C and the time to 12 minutes for the zone 2. Select AIR FRY. Select START, shaking the basket halfway through cooking. Brussels sprouts will be tender and browned when done. 10. Place sprouts in a large serving dish and drizzle with balsamic vinegar. Sprinkle bacon over top. Serve warm and immediately.

Spiced Butternut Squash and Tofu Bites

Prep time: 25 minutes | Cook time: 30 minutes | Serves 4

Spiced Butternut Squash:
600 g 1-inch-cubed butternut squash
2 tablespoons vegetable oil
1 to 2 tablespoons brown sugar
1 teaspoon Chinese five-spice powder
Tofu Bites:
1 packaged firm tofu, cubed and pressed to remove excess water
1 tablespoon soy sauce
1 tablespoon ketchup
1 tablespoon maple syrup
½ teaspoon vinegar
1 teaspoon liquid smoke
1 teaspoon hot sauce
2 tablespoons sesame seeds
1 teaspoon garlic powder
Salt and ground black pepper, to taste
Cooking spray

1. Preheat the air fryer to 180ºC. In a medium bowl, combine the squash, oil, sugar, and five-spice powder. Toss to coat. 2. Combine all the ingredients to coat the tofu completely and allow the marinade to absorb for half an hour. 3. Place the squash in the zone 1. Place the sprouts in a medium serving bowl and drizzle the sauce over the top. Toss to coat. Spritz a baking dish with cooking spray. Transfer the tofu to the zone 2. 4. Set the temeprature to 200ºC. Set the time to 15 minutes, or until tender. Select AIR FRY. Select MATCH COOK. Select START. Flip the tofu over and air fry for another 15 minutes on the other side. Serve immediately.

Stuffed Red Peppers with Herbed Ricotta-and Tomatoes-and Crispy Garlic Sliced Aubergine

Prep time: 15 minutes | Cook time: 25 minutes | Serves 4

Stuffed Red Peppers with Herbed Ricotta and Tomatoes:
2 red peppers
250 g cooked brown rice
2 plum tomatoes, diced
1 garlic clove, minced
¼ teaspoon salt
¼ teaspoon black pepper
115 g ricotta
3 tablespoons fresh basil, chopped
3 tablespoons fresh oregano, chopped
20 g shredded Parmesan, for topping
Crispy Garlic Sliced Aubergine:
1 egg
1 tablespoon water
60 g whole wheat bread crumbs
1 teaspoon garlic powder
½ teaspoon dried oregano
½ teaspoon salt
½ teaspoon paprika
1 medium aubergine, sliced into ¼-inch-thick rounds
1 tablespoon olive oil

1. Preheat the air fryer to 180ºC. 2. Cut the bell peppers in half and remove the seeds and stem. 3. In a medium bowl, combine the brown rice, tomatoes, garlic, salt, and pepper. 4. Distribute the rice filling evenly among the four bell pepper halves. 5. In a small bowl, combine the ricotta, basil, and oregano. Put the herbed cheese over the top of the rice mixture in each bell pepper. 6. In a medium shallow bowl, beat together the egg and water until frothy. 7. In a separate medium shallow bowl, mix together bread crumbs, garlic powder, oregano, salt, and paprika. 8. Dip each aubergine slice into the egg mixture, then into the bread crumb mixture, coating the outside with crumbs. 9. Place the bell peppers into the zone 1. Place the slices in a single layer in the bottom of the zone 2. Drizzle the tops of the aubergine slices with the olive oil. 10. Set the temperature to 200ºC. Set the time to 20 minutes and select ROAST for thr zone 1. Set the time to 15 minutes and select AIR FRY for the zone 2. Select START. Turn each slice and cook for an additional 10 minutes. 11. Remove and serve with shredded Parmesan on top.

Parmesan Herb Focaccia Bread and Roasted Grape Tomatoes-and-Asparagus

Prep time: 15 minutes | Cook time: 12 minutes | Serves 6

Parmesan Herb Focaccia Bread:
225 g shredded Mozzarella cheese
30 g) full-fat cream cheese
95 g blanched finely ground almond flour
40 g ground golden flaxseed
20 g grated Parmesan cheese
½ teaspoon bicarbonate of soda
2 large eggs
½ teaspoon garlic powder
¼ teaspoon dried basil
¼ teaspoon dried rosemary
2 tablespoons salted butter, melted and divided
Roasted Grape Tomatoes and Asparagus:
400 g grape tomatoes
1 bunch asparagus, trimmed
2 tablespoons olive oil
3 garlic cloves, minced
½ teaspoon coarse sea salt

1. Preheat the air fryer to 180ºC. Place Mozzarella, cream cheese, and almond flour into a large microwave-safe bowl and microwave for 1 minute. Add the flaxseed, Parmesan, and bicarbonate of soda and stir until smooth ball forms. If the mixture cools too much, it will be hard to mix. Return to microwave for 10 to 15 seconds to rewarm if necessary. 2. Stir in eggs. You may need to use your hands to get them fully incorporated. Just keep stirring and they will absorb into the dough. 3. In a large bowl, combine all of the ingredients, tossing until the vegetables are well coated with oil. 4. Sprinkle dough with garlic powder, basil, and rosemary and knead into dough. Grease a baking pan with 1 tablespoon melted butter. Press the dough evenly into the pan. Place pan into the zone 1. Pour the vegetable mixture into the zone 2 and spread into a single layer. 5. Set the temperature to 200ºC. Set the time to 10 minutes and select BAKE for the zone 1. Set the time to 7 minutes and select AIR FRY for the zone 2. Select START, cover with foil if bread begins to get too dark. 6. Remove and let cool at least 30 minutes. Drizzle with remaining butter and serve. 7.then roast for 12 minutes.

Easy Potato Croquettes and Super Cheesy Gold Aubergine

Prep time: 30 minutes | Cook time: 30 minutes

Easy Potato Croquettes | Serves 10:
55 g nutritional yeast
300 g boiled potatoes, mashed
1 flax egg
1 tablespoon flour
2 tablespoons chopped chives
Salt and ground black pepper, to taste
2 tablespoons vegetable oil
30 g bread crumbs
Super Cheesy Gold Aubergine| Serves 4:
1 medium aubergine, peeled and cut into ½-inch-thick rounds
1 teaspoon salt, plus more for seasoning
60 g plain flour
2 eggs
90 g Italian bread crumbs
2 tablespoons grated Parmesan cheese
Freshly ground black pepper, to taste
Cooking oil spray
180 g marinara sauce
45 g shredded Parmesan cheese, divided
110 g shredded Mozzarella cheese, divided

1. Preheat the air fryer to 180°C. 2. In a bowl, combine the nutritional yeast, potatoes, flax egg, flour, and chives. Sprinkle with salt and pepper as desired. 3. In a separate bowl, mix the vegetable oil and bread crumbs to achieve a crumbly consistency. 4. Shape the potato mixture into small balls and dip each one into the bread crumb mixture. 5. Put the croquettes inside the zone 1. 5. Blot the aubergine with paper towels to dry completely. You can also sprinkle with 1 teaspoon of salt to sweat out the moisture; if you do this, rinse the aubergine slices and blot dry again. 6. Place the flour in a shallow bowl. 7. In another shallow bowl, beat the eggs. 8. In a third shallow bowl, stir together the bread crumbs and grated Parmesan cheese and season with salt and pepper. 9. Dip each aubergine round in the flour, in the eggs, and into the bread crumbs to coat. 10. Insert the crisper plate into the zone 2. Once the unit is preheated, spray the crisper plate and the basket with cooking oil. Working in batches, place the aubergine rounds into the zone 2. 11. Do not stack them. Spray the aubergine with the cooking oil. 12. Set the temperature to 200°C. set the time to 15 minutes for the zone 1 and 10 minutes for the zone 2, ensuring the croquettes turn golden brown. Select AIR FRY. Select START to begin. 12. After 7 minutes, open the unit and top each round with 1 teaspoon of marinara sauce and ½ tablespoon each of shredded Parmesan and Mozzarella cheese. Resume cooking for 2 to 3 minutes until the cheese melts. 13. Repeat steps 5, 6, 7, 8, and 9 with the remaining aubergine. 14. When the cooking is complete, serve immediately.

Fried Brussels Sprouts and Southwestern Roasted Corn

Prep time: 20 minutes | Cook time: 18 minutes | Serves 4

Fried Brussels Sprouts:
1 teaspoon plus 1 tablespoon extra-virgin olive oil, divided
2 teaspoons minced garlic
2 tablespoons honey
1 tablespoon sugar
2 tablespoons freshly squeezed lemon juice
2 tablespoons rice vinegar
2 tablespoons sriracha
450 g Brussels sprouts, stems trimmed and any tough leaves removed, rinsed, halved lengthwise, and dried
½ teaspoon salt
Cooking oil spray
Southwestern Roasted Corn:
Corn:
240 g thawed frozen corn kernels
50 g diced yellow onion
150 g mixed diced bell peppers
1 jalapeño, diced
1 tablespoon fresh lemon juice
1 teaspoon ground cumin
½ teaspoon ancho chili powder
½ teaspoon coarse sea salt
For Serving:
150 g queso fresco or feta cheese
10 g chopped fresh coriander
1 tablespoon fresh lemon juice

1. Preheat the unit by selecting AIR FRY, setting the temperature to 200°C, and setting the time to 3 minutes. Select START to begin. In a small saucepan over low heat, combine 1 teaspoon of olive oil, the garlic, honey, sugar, lemon juice, vinegar, and sriracha. Cook for 2 to 3 minutes, or until slightly thickened. Remove the pan from the heat, cover, and set aside. 2. For the corn: In a large bowl, stir together the corn, onion, bell peppers, jalapeño, lemon juice, cumin, chili powder, and salt until well incorporated. 3. Place the Brussels sprouts in a resealable bag or small bowl. Add the remaining olive oil and the salt, and toss to coat. 4. Insert the crisper plate into the zone 1. Once the unit is preheated, spray the crisper plate with cooking oil. 5. Add the Brussels sprouts to the basket. Pour the spiced vegetables into the zone 2. 6. Set the temperature to 190°C for 10 minutes for the zone 1, stirring halfway through the cooking time. Set the temperature to 200°C for 15 minutes for the zone 2. Select AIR FRY. Select START to begin. 7. After 7 or 8 minutes, remove the basket and shake it to toss the sprouts. Reinsert the basket to resume cooking. 8. Place the sprouts in a medium serving bowl and drizzle the sauce over the top. Toss to coat. 9. When the cooking is complete, the leaves should be crispy and light brown and the sprout centres tender. 10. Transfer the corn mixture to a serving bowl. Add the cheese, coriander, and lemon juice and stir well to combine. Serve immediately.

Spicy Roasted Bok Choy and Maple-Roasted Tomatoes

Prep time: 25 minutes | Cook time: 20 minutes | Serves 4

Spicy Roasted Bok Choy:
2 tablespoons olive oil
2 tablespoons reduced-sodium coconut aminos
2 teaspoons sesame oil
2 teaspoons chili-garlic sauce
2 cloves garlic, minced
1 head (about 450 g) bok choy, sliced lengthwise into quarters
2 teaspoons black sesame seeds

Maple-Roasted Tomatoes | Serves 2:
280 g cherry tomatoes, halved
coarse sea salt, to taste
2 tablespoons maple syrup
1 tablespoon vegetable oil
2 sprigs fresh thyme, stems removed
1 garlic clove, minced
Freshly ground black pepper

1. Preheat the air fryer to 180°C. 2. In a large bowl, combine the olive oil, coconut aminos, sesame oil, chili-garlic sauce, and garlic. Add the bok choy and toss, massaging the leaves with your hands if necessary, until thoroughly coated. 3. Place the tomatoes in a colander and sprinkle liberally with salt. Let stand for 10 minutes to drain. 4. Transfer the tomatoes cut-side up to a cake pan, then drizzle with the maple syrup, followed by the oil. Sprinkle with the thyme leaves and garlic and season with pepper. Place the pan in the zone 1. Arrange the bok choy in the zone 2 of the air fryer. Pausing about halfway through the cooking time to shake the basket. 5. Set the temeprature to 160°C for 20 minutes for the zone 1 until the tomatoes are soft, collapsed, and lightly caramelized on top. Set the temepratureto 200°C for 7 to 10 minutes until the bok choy is tender and the tips of the leaves begin to crisp. Select ROAST for the zone 1 and AIR FRY for the zone 2. Select START. 6. Remove from the basket and let cool for a few minutes before coarsely chopping. Serve sprinkled with the sesame seeds. 7. Serve straight from the pan or transfer the tomatoes to a plate and drizzle with the juices from the pan to serve.

Spinach-and-Cheese Stuffed Tomatoes and Simple Cougette Crisps

Prep time: 25 minutes | Cook time: 15 minutes

Spinach and Cheese Stuffed Tomatoes | Serves 2:
4 ripe beefsteak tomatoes
¾ teaspoon black pepper
½ teaspoon coarse sea salt
1 (280 g) package frozen chopped spinach, thawed and squeezed dry
1 (150 g) package garlic-and-herb Boursin cheese
3 tablespoons sour cream
45 g finely grated Parmesan cheese

Simple Cougette Crisps | Serves 4:
2 courgette, sliced into ¼- to ½-inch-thick rounds
¼ teaspoon garlic granules
⅛ teaspoon sea salt
Freshly ground black pepper, to taste (optional)
Cooking spray

1. Preheat the air fryer to 180°C. Cut the tops off the tomatoes. Using a small spoon, carefully remove and discard the pulp. Season the insides with ½ teaspoon of the black pepper and ¼ teaspoon of the salt. Invert the tomatoes onto paper towels and allow to drain while you make the filling. 2. Meanwhile, in a medium bowl, combine the spinach, Boursin cheese, sour cream, ½ of the Parmesan, and the remaining ¼ teaspoon salt and ¼ teaspoon pepper. Stir until ingredients are well combined. Divide the filling among the tomatoes. Top with the remaining ½ of the Parmesan. 3. Place the tomatoes in the zone 1. Put the courgette rounds in the zone 2, spreading them out as much as possible. Top with a sprinkle of garlic granules, sea salt, and black pepper (if desired). Spritz the courgette rounds with cooking spray. 4. Set the temperature to 180°C and select AIR FRY for 15 minutes for the zone 1, or until the filling is hot. Set the temperature to 200°C and select ROAST for 14 minutes for the zone 2. Select START. 5. Spritz the zone 2 with cooking spray, flipping the courgette rounds halfway through, or until the courgette rounds are crisp-tender. 6. Let them rest for 5 minutes and serve.

Chapter 9 Vegetarian Mains

Chapter 9 Vegetarian Mains

Cauliflower, Chickpea, and Avocado Mash and Air Fryer Veggies with Halloumi

Prep time: 15 minutes | Cook time: 25 minutes | Serves 4

Cauliflower, Chickpea, and Avocado Mash:
1 medium head cauliflower, cut into florets
1 can chickpeas, drained and rinsed
1 tablespoon extra-virgin olive oil
2 tablespoons lemon juice
Salt and ground black pepper, to taste
4 flatbreads, toasted
2 ripe avocados, mashed
Air Fryer Veggies with Halloumi | Serves 2:
2 courgettes, cut into even chunks
1 large aubergine, peeled, cut into chunks
1 large carrot, cut into chunks
170 g halloumi cheese, cubed
2 teaspoons olive oil
Salt and black pepper, to taste
1 teaspoon dried mixed herbs

1. Preheat the air fryer to 180°C. In a bowl, mix the chickpeas, cauliflower, lemon juice and olive oil. Sprinkle salt and pepper as desired. Put inside the zone 1. 2. Combine the courgettes, aubergine, carrot, cheese, olive oil, salt, and pepper in a large bowl and toss to coat well. Spread the mixture evenly in the zone 2. 3. Set the temperature to 200°C. Set the time to 25 minutes for the zone 1 and 14 minutes for the zone 2 until crispy and golden. Select AIR FRY. Select START. 4. Spread on top of the flatbread along with the mashed avocado. Sprinkle with more pepper and salt and serve, shaking the basket once during cooking. Serve topped with mixed herbs.

Baked Turnip-and-Courgette and Courgette-and-Spinach Croquettes

Prep time: 14 minutes | Cook time: 15 minutes | Serves 4

Baked Turnip and Courgette:
3 turnips, sliced
1 large courgette, sliced
1 large red onion, cut into rings
2 cloves garlic, crushed
1 tablespoon olive oil
Salt and black pepper, to taste
Courgette and Spinach Croquettes | Serves 6:
4 eggs, slightly beaten
120 ml almond flour
120 ml goat cheese, crumbled
1 teaspoon fine sea salt
4 garlic cloves, minced
235 ml baby spinach
120 ml Parmesan cheese, grated
⅓ teaspoon red pepper flakes
450 g courgette, peeled and grated
⅓ teaspoon dried dill weed

1. Preheat the air fryer to 180°C. Put the turnips, courgette, red onion, and garlic in a baking pan. Drizzle the olive oil over the top and sprinkle with the salt and pepper. 2. Place the baking pan in the preheated zone 1. Thoroughly combine all ingredients in a bowl. Now, roll the mixture to form small croquettes in the zone 2. 3. Set the temperature to 200°C for 15 to 20 minutes foor the zone 1, or until the vegetables are tender. Set the temperature to 170°C for 7 minutes for the zone 2 or until golden. Select Bake for the zone 1 and AIR FRY for the zone 2. Select START. 4. Remove from the basket and serve on a plate. Tate, adjust for seasonings and serve warm.

Caprese Aubergine Stacks and Cheese Stuffed Courgette

Prep time: 25 minutes | Cook time: 12 minutes | Serves 4

Caprese Aubergine Stacks:
1 medium aubergine, cut into ¼-inch slices
2 large tomatoes, cut into ¼-inch slices
110 g fresh Mozzarella, cut into 14 g slices
2 tablespoons olive oil
60 ml fresh basil, sliced
Cheese Stuffed Courgette:
1 large courgette, cut into four pieces
2 tablespoons olive oil
235 ml Ricotta cheese, room temperature
2 tablespoons spring onions, chopped
1 heaping tablespoon fresh parsley, roughly chopped
1 heaping tablespoon coriander, minced
60 g Cheddar cheese, preferably freshly grated
1 teaspoon celery seeds
½ teaspoon salt
½ teaspoon garlic pepper

1. In a baking dish, place four slices of aubergine on the bottom. 2. Place a slice of tomato on top of each aubergine round, then Mozzarella, then aubergine. Repeat as necessary. Drizzle with olive oil. Cover dish with foil and place dish into the zone 1. Put the courgette in the zone 2. 3. Set the temperature to 180°C. Set the time to 12 minutes for the zone 1 and 10 minutes for zone 2. Select BAKE. Select START. 4. Check for doneness and cook for 2-3 minutes longer if needed. When done, aubergine will be tender. Garnish with fresh basil to serve. 5. Meanwhile, make the stuffing by mixing the other items. When your courgette is thoroughly cooked, open them up. Divide the stuffing among all courgette pieces and bake an additional 5 minutes.

Italian Baked Egg and Veggies and Pesto Spinach Flatbread

Prep time: 20 minutes | Cook time: 10 minutes | Serves 2

Italian Baked Egg and Veggies:
2 tablespoons salted butter
1 small courgette, sliced lengthwise and quartered
½ medium green pepper, seeded and diced
235 ml fresh spinach, chopped
1 medium plum tomato, diced
2 large eggs
¼ teaspoon onion powder
¼ teaspoon garlic powder
½ teaspoon dried basil
¼ teaspoon dried oregano
Pesto Spinach Flatbread | Serves 4
235 ml blanched finely ground almond flour
60 g soft white cheese
475 ml shredded Mozzarella cheese
235 ml chopped fresh spinach leaves
2 tablespoons basil pesto

1. Grease two ramekins with 1 tablespoon butter each. In a large bowl, toss courgette, pepper, spinach, and tomato. 2. Place flour, soft white cheese, and Mozzarella in a large microwave-safe bowl and microwave on high 45 seconds, then stir. 3. Fold in spinach and microwave an additional 15 seconds. Stir until a soft dough ball forms. 4. Divide the mixture in two and place half in each ramekin. Crack an egg on top of each ramekin and sprinkle with onion powder, garlic powder, basil, and oregano. Place into the zone 1. 5. Cut two pieces of parchment paper to fit zone 2. 6. Separate dough into two sections and press each out on ungreased parchment to create 6-inch rounds. Spread 1 tablespoon pesto over each flatbread and place rounds on parchment into ungreased zone 2. 7. Set the temperature to 170ºC and select BAKE for 10 minutes for the zone 1. Set the temperature to 180ºC and select AIR FRY for 8 minutes for the zone 2, turning crusts halfway through cooking. Select START. 8. Flatbread will be golden when done. Let cool 5 minutes before slicing and serving.

Mushroom and Pepper Pizza Squares

Prep time: 10 minutes | Cook time: 10 minutes | Serves 10

1 pizza dough, cut into squares
235 ml chopped oyster mushrooms
1 shallot, chopped
¼ red pepper, chopped
2 tablespoons parsley
Salt and ground black pepper, to taste

1. Preheat the air fryer to 180ºC. In a bowl, combine the oyster mushrooms, shallot, pepper and parsley. 2. Sprinkle some salt and pepper as desired. Spread this mixture on top of the pizza squares. Put the pizza in the dual zone air fry. 3. Set the temeprature to 180ºC and the time to 10 minutes. Select START. Serve warm.

Garlic White Courgette Rolls and Crispy Tofu

Prep time: 50 minutes | Cook time: 20 minutes | Serves 4

2 medium courgette
2 tablespoons unsalted butter
¼ white onion, peeled and diced
½ teaspoon finely minced roasted garlic
60 ml double cream
2 tablespoons vegetable broth
⅛ teaspoon xanthan gum
120 ml full-fat ricotta cheese
¼ teaspoon salt
½ teaspoon garlic powder
¼ teaspoon dried oregano
475 ml spinach, chopped
120 ml sliced baby portobello mushrooms
180 ml shredded Mozzarella cheese, divided
Crispy Tofu:
1 (454 g) block extra-firm tofu
2 tablespoons coconut aminos
1 tablespoon toasted sesame oil
1 tablespoon olive oil
1 tablespoon chilli-garlic sauce
1½ teaspoons black sesame seeds
1 spring onion, thinly sliced

1. Preheat the air fryer to 180ºC. Using a mandoline or sharp knife, slice courgette into long strips lengthwise. Place strips between paper towels to absorb moisture. Set aside. 2. In a medium saucepan over medium heat, melt butter. Add onion and sauté until fragrant. Add garlic and sauté 30 seconds. Pour in double cream, broth, and xanthan gum. 3. Turn off heat and whisk mixture until it begins to thicken, about 3 minutes. 4. In a medium bowl, add ricotta, salt, garlic powder, and oregano and mix well. Fold in spinach, mushrooms, and 120 ml Mozzarella. Pour half of the sauce into a round baking pan. To assemble the rolls, place two strips of courgette on a work surface. Spoon 2 tablespoons of ricotta mixture onto the slices and roll up. 5. Place seam side down on top of sauce. Repeat with remaining ingredients. Pour remaining sauce over the rolls and sprinkle with remaining Mozzarella. Cover with foil and place into zone 1. 6. Press the tofu for at least 15 minutes by wrapping it in paper towels and setting a heavy pan on top so that the moisture drains. 7. Slice the tofu into bite-size cubes and transfer to a bowl. Drizzle with the coconut aminos, sesame oil, olive oil, and chilli-garlic sauce. 8. Cover and refrigerate for 1 hour or up to overnight. 9. Arrange the tofu in a single layer in the zone 2. Pausing to shake the pan halfway through the cooking time, 6. Set the temperature to 180ºC for 20 minutes for the zone 1. and bake. Set the temperature to 180ºC for 15 to 20 minutes for the zone 2 until crisp. Select BAKE for the zone 1 and AIR FRY for the zone 2. Select START. 7. In the last 5 minutes, remove the foil to brown the cheese. 8. Serve with any juices that accumulate in the bottom of the air fryer, sprinkled with the sesame seeds and sliced spring onion. Serve immediately.

Cheesy Cauliflower Pizza Crust and Broccoli-Cheese Fritters

Prep time: 20 minutes | Cook time: 20 minutes

Cheesy Cauliflower Pizza Crust | Serves 2:
1 (340 g) steamer bag cauliflower
120 ml shredded extra mature Cheddar cheese
1 large egg
2 tablespoons blanched finely ground almond flour
1 teaspoon Italian blend seasoning
Broccoli-Cheese Fritters | Serves 4:
235 ml broccoli florets
235 ml shredded Mozzarella cheese
180 ml almond flour
120 ml milled flaxseed, divided
2 teaspoons baking powder
1 teaspoon garlic powder
Salt and freshly ground black pepper, to taste
2 eggs, lightly beaten
120 ml ranch dressing

1. Preheat the air fryer to 180°C. Cook cauliflower according to package instructions. Remove from bag and place into cheesecloth or paper towel to remove excess water. 2. Place cauliflower into a large bowl. Add cheese, egg, almond flour, and Italian seasoning to the bowl and mix well. Cut a piece of parchment to fit your air fryer basket. Press cauliflower into 6-inch round circle. Place into the zone 1. 3. In a food processor fitted with a metal blade, pulse the broccoli until very finely chopped. 2. Transfer the broccoli to a large bowl and add the Mozzarella, almond flour, 60 ml milled flaxseed, baking powder, and garlic powder. 4. Stir until thoroughly combined. Season to taste with salt and black pepper. Add the eggs and stir again to form a sticky dough. Shape the dough into 1¼-inch fritters. 5. Place the remaining 60 ml milled flaxseed in a shallow bowl and roll the fritters in the meal to form an even coating. 6. Working in batches if necessary, arrange the fritters in a single layer in the basket of the dual zone air fryer and spray generously with olive oil. 7. Set the temperature to 180°C for 11 minutes for the zone 1. After 7 minutes, flip the pizza crust. Add preferred toppings to pizza. Set the temperature to 200°C for 20 to 25 minutes for the zone 2 until the fritters are golden brown and crispy. Select AIR FRY. Select START. 8. Place back into zone 1 and cook an additional 4 minutes or until fully cooked and golden. 9. Serve with the ranch dressing for dipping. Pausing halfway through the cooking time to shake the basket. Serve immediately.

Loaded Cauliflower Steak and Aubergine and Courgette Bites

Prep time: 35 minutes | Cook time: 30 minutes | Serves 4

1 medium head cauliflower
60 ml hot sauce
2 tablespoons salted butter, melted
60 ml blue cheese, crumbled
60 ml full-fat ranch dressing
Aubergine and Courgette Bites | Serves 8:
2 teaspoons fresh mint leaves, chopped
1½ teaspoons red pepper chilli flakes
2 tablespoons melted butter
450 g aubergine, peeled and cubed
450 g courgette, peeled and cubed
3 tablespoons olive oil

1. Remove cauliflower leaves. Slice the head in ½-inch-thick slices. 2. In a small bowl, mix hot sauce and butter. Brush the mixture over the cauliflower. 3. Place each cauliflower steak into the zone 1, working in batches if necessary. Toss all the above ingredients in a large-sized mixing dish in the zone 2. 4. Set the temperature to 200°C for 7 minutes for the zone 1. Set the temperature to 160°C for 30 minutes for the zone 2. Select AIR FRY for the zone 1 and AIR FRY for the zone 2. Select START, turning once or twice. When cooked, edges will begin turning dark and caramelized. 5. To serve, sprinkle steaks with crumbled blue cheese. Drizzle with ranch dressing. Serve with a homemade dipping sauce.

Chapter 10 Desserts

Chapter 10 Desserts

Cinnamon Cupcakes with Cream Cheese Frosting and Zucchini Bread

Prep time: 20 minutes | Cook time: 40 minutes

Cinnamon Cupcakes with Cream Cheese Frosting | Serves 6:
- 50 g almond flour, plus 2 tablespoons
- 2 tablespoons low-carb vanilla protein powder
- ⅛ teaspoon salt
- 1 teaspoon baking powder
- ¼ teaspoon ground cinnamon
- 55 g unsalted butter
- 25 g powdered sweetener
- 2 eggs
- ½ teaspoon vanilla extract
- 2 tablespoons heavy cream

Cream Cheese Frosting:
- 110 g cream cheese, softened
- 2 tablespoons unsalted butter, softened
- ½ teaspoon vanilla extract
- 2 tablespoons powdered sweetener
- 1 to 2 tablespoons heavy cream

Zucchini Bread | Serves 12:
- 220 g coconut flour
- 2 teaspoons baking powder
- 150 g granulated sweetener
- 120 ml coconut oil, melted
- 1 teaspoon apple cider vinegar
- 1 teaspoon vanilla extract
- 3 eggs, beaten
- 1 courgette, grated
- 1 teaspoon ground cinnamon

Preheat the air fryer to 180°C. Lightly coat 6 silicone muffin cups with oil and set aside. 2. In a medium bowl, combine the almond flour, protein powder, salt, baking powder, and cinnamon; set aside. 3. In a stand mixer fitted with a paddle attachment, beat the butter and sweetener until creamy. Add the eggs, vanilla, and heavy cream, and beat again until thoroughly combined. Add half the flour mixture at a time to the butter mixture, mixing after each addition, until you have a smooth, creamy batter. 4. Divide the batter evenly among the muffin cups, filling each one about three-fourths full. Arrange the muffin cups in the zone 1. 5. In the mixing bowl, mix coconut flour with baking powder, sweetener, coconut oil, apple cider vinegar, vanilla extract, eggs, courgette, and ground cinnamon. 6. Transfer the mixture into the zone 2 and flatten it in the shape of the bread. 7. Set the temperature to 200°C for 20 to 25 minutes for the zone 1, or until a toothpick inserted into the center of a cupcake comes out clean. Set the temperature to 180°C for 40 minutes for the zone 2. Select AIR FRY. Select START. 8. Transfer the cupcakes to a rack and let cool completely. 9. To make the cream cheese frosting: In a stand mixer fitted with a paddle attachment, beat the cream cheese, butter, and vanilla until fluffy. Add the sweetener and mix again until thoroughly combined. With the mixer running, add the heavy cream a tablespoon at a time until the frosting is smooth and creamy. Frost the cupcakes as desired.

Brown Sugar Banana Bread and Hazelnut Butter Cookies

Prep time: 50 minutes | Cook time: 22 minutes | Serves 4

- 195 g packed light brown sugar
- 1 large egg, beaten
- 2 tablespoons unsalted butter, melted
- 120 ml milk, whole or semi-skimmed
- 250 g plain flour
- 1½ teaspoons baking powder
- 1 teaspoon ground cinnamon
- ½ teaspoon salt
- 1 banana, mashed
- 1 to 2 tablespoons coconut, or avocado oil oil
- 30 g icing sugar (optional)

Hazelnut Butter Cookies| Serves 10:
- 4 tablespoons liquid monk fruit, or agave syrup
- 65 g hazelnuts, ground
- 110 g unsalted butter, room temperature
- 190 g almond flour
- 110 g coconut flour
- 55 g granulated sweetener
- 2 teaspoons ground cinnamon

1.Preheat the air fryer to 180°C. In a large bowl, stir together the brown sugar, egg, melted butter, and milk. 2. In a medium bowl, whisk the flour, baking powder, cinnamon, and salt until blended. Add the flour mixture to the sugar mixture and stir just to blend. 3. Add the mashed banana and stir to combine. 4. Spritz 2 mini loaf pans with oil. 5. Cream liquid monk fruit with butter until the mixture becomes fluffy. Sift in both types of flour. 6. Now, stir in the hazelnuts. Now, knead the mixture to form a dough; place in the refrigerator for about 35 minutes. 7. To finish, shape the prepared dough into the bite-sized balls; arrange them on a dual zone baking dish; flatten the balls using the back of a spoon. 8. Mix granulated sweetener with ground cinnamon. 9. Evenly divide the batter between the prepared pans and place them in the zone 1. Press your cookies in the cinnamon mixture until they are completely covered. Put the cookies in the zone 2. 10. Set the temperature to 200°C for 22 to 24 minutes for the zone 1, or until a knife inserted into the middle of the loaves comes out clean. Set the temperature to 200°C for 20 minutes for the zone 2. Select BAKE. Select START. 11. Dust the warm loaves with icing sugar (if using). Leave them to cool for about 10 minutes before transferring them to a wire rack. Bon appétit!

Coconut Mixed Berry Crisp and Peanut Butter, Honey & Banana Toast

Prep time: 15 minutes | Cook time: 20 minutes | Serves 6

Coconut Mixed Berry Crisp :
1 tablespoon butter, melted
340 g mixed berries
65 g granulated sweetener
1 teaspoon pure vanilla extract
½ teaspoon ground cinnamon
¼ teaspoon ground cloves
¼ teaspoon grated nutmeg
50 g coconut chips, for garnish
Peanut Butter, Honey & Banana
Toast | Serves 4 :
2 tablespoons unsalted butter, softened
4 slices white bread
4 tablespoons peanut butter
2 bananas, peeled and thinly sliced
4 tablespoons honey
1 teaspoon ground cinnamon

1. Preheat the air fryer to 180°C. Coat a baking pan with melted butter. 2. Put the remaining ingredients except the coconut chips in the prepared zone 1. 3. Cut each slice in half lengthwise so that it will better fit into the zone 2. Arrange two pieces of bread, butter sides down, in the zone 2. 3. Set the temperature 190°C and select BAKE for 20 minutes for the zone 1. Set the temperature to 190°C and select AIR FRY for 5 minutes for the zone 2. Select START. Then cook for an additional 4 minutes, or until the bananas have started to brown. Repeat with remaining slices. 4. Serve garnished with the coconut chips. 5. Spread butter on one side of each slice of bread, then peanut butter on the other side. Arrange the banana slices on top of the peanut butter sides of each slice (about 9 slices per toast). Drizzle honey on top of the banana and sprinkle with cinnamon. Serve hot.

Blackberry Peach Cobbler with Vanilla and Honeyed, Roasted Apples with Walnuts

Prep time: 15 minutes | Cook time: 20 minutes | Serves 4

Filling:
170 g blackberries
250 g chopped peaches, cut into ½-inch thick slices
2 teaspoons arrowroot or cornflour
2 tablespoons coconut sugar
1 teaspoon lemon juice
Topping:
2 tablespoons sunflower oil
1 tablespoon maple syrup
1 teaspoon vanilla
3 tablespoons coconut sugar
40 g rolled oats
45 g whole-wheat pastry, or
plain flour
1 teaspoon cinnamon
¼ teaspoon nutmeg
⅛ teaspoon sea salt
Roasted Apples with Walnuts | Serves 4:
2 Granny Smith apples
20 g certified gluten-free rolled oats
2 tablespoons honey
½ teaspoon ground cinnamon
2 tablespoons chopped walnuts
Pinch salt
1 tablespoon olive oil

1. Preheat the air fryer to 180°C. Combine the blackberries, peaches, arrowroot, coconut sugar, and lemon juice in a baking pan. 2. Using a rubber spatula, stir until well incorporated. Set aside. 3. Combine the oil, maple syrup, and vanilla in a mixing bowl and stir well. Whisk in the remaining ingredients. Spread this mixture evenly over the filling. 4. Core the apples and slice them in half. 5. In a medium bowl, mix together the oats, honey, cinnamon, walnuts, salt, and olive oil. 6. Scoop a quarter of the oat mixture onto the top of each half apple. 7. Place the pan in the zone 1 and place the apples in the zone 2. 8. Set the temperature to 200°C. Set the time to 20 minutes and select BAKE for the zone 1, or until the topping is crispy and golden brown. 9. Set the time to 12 to 15 minutes and select ROAST for the zone 2, or until the apples are fork tender. Select START. Serve warm.

Mini Peanut Butter Tarts

Prep time: 25 minutes | Cook time: 12 to 15 minutes | Serves 8

125 g pecans
110 g finely ground blanched almond flour
2 tablespoons unsalted butter, at room temperature
50 g powdered sweetener, plus 2 tablespoons, divided
120 g heavy (whipping) cream
2 tablespoons mascarpone
cheese
110 g cream cheese
140 g sugar-free peanut butter
1 teaspoon pure vanilla extract
⅛ teaspoon sea salt
85 g organic chocolate chips
1 tablespoon coconut oil
40 g chopped peanuts or pecans

1. Place the pecans in the bowl of a food processor; process until they are finely ground. 2. Transfer the ground pecans to a medium bowl and stir in the almond flour. Add the butter and 2 tablespoons of sweetener and stir until the mixture becomes wet and crumbly. 3. Divide the mixture among 8 silicone muffin cups, pressing the crust firmly with your fingers into the bottom and part way up the sides of each cup. 4. Arrange the muffin cups in the zone 1, working in batches if necessary. Set the temperature to 150°C. Set the time to 12 to 15 minutes. Select BAKE. Select MATCH COOK. Select START. Until the crusts begin to brown. Remove the cups from the air fryer and set them aside to cool. 5. In the bowl of a stand mixer, combine the heavy cream and mascarpone cheese. Beat until peaks form. Transfer to a large bowl. 6. In the same stand mixer bowl, combine the cream cheese, peanut butter, remaining 50 g sweetener, vanilla, and salt. Beat at medium-high speed until smooth. 7. Reduce the speed to low and add the heavy cream mixture back a spoonful at a time, beating after each addition. 8. Spoon the peanut butter mixture over the crusts and freeze the tarts for 30 minutes. 9. Place the chocolate chips and coconut oil in the top of a double boiler over high heat. Stir until melted, then remove from the heat. 10. Drizzle the melted chocolate over the peanut butter tarts. Top with the chopped nuts and freeze the tarts for another 15 minutes, until set. 11. Store the peanut butter tarts in an airtight container in the refrigerator for up to 1 week or in the freezer for up to 1 month.

Coconut-Custard Pie and Pears with Honey-Lemon Ricotta

Prep time: 10 minutes | Cook time: 20 minutes | Serves 4

Coconut-Custard Pie :
240 ml milk
50 g granulated sugar, plus 2 tablespoons
30 g scone mix
1 teaspoon vanilla extract
2 eggs
2 tablespoons melted butter
Cooking spray
50 g desiccated, sweetened coconut
Pears with Honey-Lemon Ricotta | Serves 4:
2 large Bartlett pears
3 tablespoons butter, melted
3 tablespoons brown sugar
½ teaspoon ground ginger
¼ teaspoon ground cardamom
125 g full-fat ricotta cheese
1 tablespoon honey, plus additional for drizzling
1 teaspoon pure almond extract
1 teaspoon pure lemon extract

1. Preheat the air fryer to 180°C. Place all ingredients except coconut in a medium bowl. 2. Using a hand mixer, beat on high speed for 3 minutes. 3. Let sit for 5 minutes. 4. Spray a baking pan with cooking spray and place pan in the zone 1. 5. Pour filling into pan and sprinkle coconut over top. Put the pie in the zone 1. 6. Peel each pear and cut in half, lengthwise. Use a melon baller to scoop out the core. Place the pear halves in a medium bowl, add the melted butter, and toss. Add the brown sugar, ginger, and cardamom; toss to coat. 7. Place the pear halves, cut side down, in the zone 2. 8. Set the temperature to 190°C and select BAKE for 20 to 23 minutes for the zone 1o until center sets. Set the temperature to 190°C and select AIR FRY for 8 to 10 minutes for the zone 2, or until the pears are lightly browned and tender, but not mushy. Select START. 9. Meanwhile, in a medium bowl, combine the ricotta, honey, and almond and lemon extracts. Beat with an electric mixer on medium speed until the mixture is light and fluffy, about 1 minute. 10. To serve, divide the ricotta mixture among four small shallow bowls. Place a pear half, cut side up, on top of the cheese. Drizzle with additional honey and serve.

Glazed Cherry Turnovers

Prep time: 10 minutes | Cook time: 14 minutes per batch | Serves 8

2 sheets frozen puff pastry, thawed
600 g can premium cherry pie filling
2 teaspoons ground cinnamon
1 egg, beaten
90 g sliced almonds
120 g icing sugar
2 tablespoons milk

1. Preheat the air fryer to 180°C. Roll a sheet of puff pastry out into a square that is approximately 10-inches by 10-inches. Cut this large square into quarters. 2. Mix the cherry pie filling and cinnamon together in a bowl. Spoon ¼ cup of the cherry filling into the center of each puff pastry square. 3. Brush the perimeter of the pastry square with the egg wash. Fold one corner of the puff pastry over the cherry pie filling towards the opposite corner, forming a triangle. 4. Seal the two edges of the pastry together with the tip of a fork, making a design with the tines. Brush the top of the turnovers with the egg wash and sprinkle sliced almonds over each one. Repeat these steps with the second sheet of puff pastry. You should have eight turnovers at the end. 5. Set the temperature to 200°C. Set the time to 14 minutes. Select BAKE. Select MATCH COOK. Select START, carefully turning them over halfway through the cooking time. 6. While the turnovers are cooking, make the glaze by whisking the icing sugar and milk together in a small bowl until smooth. Let the glaze sit for a minute so the sugar can absorb the milk. If the consistency is still too thick to drizzle, add a little more milk, a drop at a time, and stir until smooth. 7. Let the cooked cherry turnovers sit for at least 10 minutes. Then drizzle the glaze over each turnover in a zigzag motion. Serve warm or at room temperature.

Almond Shortbread and Crispy Pineapple Rings

Prep time: 15 minutes | Cook time: 12 minutes | Serves 8

110 g unsalted butter
100 g granulated sugar
1 teaspoon pure almond extract
125 g plain flour
Crispy Pineapple Rings | Serves 6:
240 ml rice milk
85 g plain flour
120 ml water
25 g unsweetened flaked coconut
4 tablespoons granulated sugar
½ teaspoon baking soda
½ teaspoon baking powder
½ teaspoon vanilla essence
½ teaspoon ground cinnamon
¼ teaspoon ground star anise
Pinch of kosher, or coarse sea salt
1 medium pineapple, peeled and sliced

1. Preheat the air fryer to 180°C. In bowl of a stand mixer fitted with the paddle attachment, beat the butter and sugar on medium speed until light and fluffy (3 to 4 minutes). Add the almond extract and beat until combined (about 30 seconds). Turn the mixer to low. Add the flour a little at a time and beat for about 2 minutes more until well-incorporated. 2. In a large bowl, stir together all the ingredients except the pineapple. 3. Dip each pineapple slice into the batter until evenly coated. 3. Pat the dough into an even layer in a baking pan. Place the pan in the zone 1. Arrange the pineapple slices in the zone 2. 4. Set the temperature to 190°C and select bake for 12 minutes for the zone 1. Set the temperature to 200° and select AIR FRY for 6 to 8 minutes for the zone 2 until golden brown. Select START. 5. Carefully remove the pan from air fryer basket. While the shortbread is still warm and soft, cut it into 8 wedges. 6. Let cool in the pan on a wire rack for 5 minutes. Remove the wedges from the pan and let cool completely on the rack before serving.

Chocolate and Rum Cupcakes and Air Fryer Apple Fritters

Prep time: 35 minutes | Cook time: 15 minutes

Chocolate and Rum Cupcakes:
150 g granulated sweetener
140 g almond flour
1 teaspoon unsweetened baking powder
3 teaspoons cocoa powder
½ teaspoon baking soda
½ teaspoon ground cinnamon
¼ teaspoon grated nutmeg
⅛ teaspoon salt
120 ml milk
110 g butter, at room temperature
3 eggs, whisked
1 teaspoon pure rum extract
70 g blueberries
Cooking spray
Air Fryer Apple Fritters:
1 chopped, peeled Granny Smith apple
115 g granulated sugar
1 teaspoon ground cinnamon
120 g plain flour
1 teaspoon baking powder
1 teaspoon salt
2 tablespoons milk
2 tablespoons butter, melted
1 large egg, beaten
Cooking spray
25 g icing sugar (optional)

1.Preheat the air fryer to 180°C. Spray a 6-cup muffin tin with cooking spray. 2. In a mixing bowl, combine the sweetener, almond flour, baking powder, cocoa powder, baking soda, cinnamon, nutmeg, and salt and stir until well blended. 3. In another mixing bowl, mix together the milk, butter, egg, and rum extract until thoroughly combined. Slowly and carefully pour this mixture into the bowl of dry mixture. Stir in the blueberries. Put them in the zone 1. 4. Mix together the apple, granulated sugar, and cinnamon in a small bowl. Allow to sit for 30 minutes. 5. Combine the flour, baking powder, and salt in a medium bowl. Add the milk, butter, and egg and stir to incorporate. 6. Pour the apple mixture into the bowl of flour mixture and stir with a spatula until a dough forms. 7. Make the fritters: On a clean work surface, divide the dough into 12 equal portions and shape into 1-inch balls. Flatten them into patties with your hands. 8. Spoon the batter into the greased muffin cups, filling each about three-quarters full. 9. Line the zone 2 with baking paper and spray it with cooking spray. 10. Transfer the apple fritters onto the baking paper, evenly spaced but not too close together. Spray the fritters with cooking spray. 11. Set the temperature to 200°C. Set the time to 15 minutes for the zone 1 and 7 to 8 minutes for the zone 2 until lightly browned, or until the center is springy and a toothpick inserted in the middle comes out clean. Select BAKE. Select START. Flip the fritters halfway through the cooking time. 12. Remove from the basket and place on a wire rack to cool. 13. Remove from the basket to a plate and serve with the confectioners' sugar sprinkled on top, if desired.

Indian Toast-and-Milk and Rhubarb-and-Strawberry Crumble

Prep time: 20 minutes | Cook time: 20 minutes | Serves 4

305 g sweetened, condensed milk
240 ml evaporated milk
240 ml single cream
1 teaspoon ground cardamom, plus additional for garnish
1 pinch saffron threads
4 slices white bread
2 to 3 tablespoons ghee or butter, softened
2 tablespoons crushed pistachios, for garnish (optional)
Rhubarb and Strawberry Crumble| Serves 6:
250 g sliced fresh strawberries
95 g sliced rhubarb
75 g granulated sugar
60 g quick-cooking oatmeal
50 g whole-wheat pastry flour, or plain flour
50 g packed light brown sugar
½ teaspoon ground cinnamon
3 tablespoons unsalted butter, melted

1.In a baking pan, combine the condensed milk, evaporated milk, half-and-half, cardamom, and saffron. Stir until well combined. 2. Place the pan in the air fryer basket. Set the air fryer to 180°C for 15 minutes, stirring halfway through the cooking time. Remove the sweetened milk from the air fryer and set aside. 3. Insert the crisper plate into the zone 2 and the basket into the unit. 4. In a 6-by-2-inch round metal baking pan, combine the strawberries, rhubarb, and granulated sugar. 5. In a medium bowl, stir together the oatmeal, flour, brown sugar, and cinnamon. Stir the melted butter into this mixture until crumbly. Sprinkle the crumble mixture over the fruit. 6. Cut each slice of bread into two triangles. Brush each side with ghee. Place the bread in the zone 1. 6. Garnish with pistachios if using, and sprinkle with additional cardamom. 7. Once the unit is preheated, place the pan into zone 2. 8. Set the temperature to 180°C and select AIR FRY for 5 minutes for the zone 1 or until golden brown and toasty. Set the temperature to 200°C and select BAKE for 12 minutes for the zone 2. Select START, then check the crumble. If the fruit is bubbling and the topping is golden brown, it is done. If not, resume cooking. 9. Remove the bread from the air fryer. Arrange two triangles in each of four wide, shallow bowls. Pour the hot milk mixture on top of the bread and let soak for 30 minutes. 10. When the cooking is complete, serve warm.

Strawberry Shortcake and Crumbly Coconut-Pecan Cookies

Prep time: 20 minutes | Cook time: 25 minutes

Strawberry Shortcake | Serves 6:
2 tablespoons coconut oil
110 g blanched finely ground almond flour
2 large eggs, whisked
100 g granulated sweetener
1 teaspoon baking powder
1 teaspoon vanilla extract
240 g heavy cream, whipped
6 medium fresh strawberries, hulled and sliced
Crumbly Coconut-Pecan Cookies | Serves 10:
170 g coconut flour
170 g extra-fine almond flour
½ teaspoon baking powder
⅓ teaspoon baking soda
3 eggs plus an egg yolk, beaten
175 ml coconut oil, at room temperature
125 g unsalted pecan nuts, roughly chopped
150 g monk fruit, or equivalent sweetener
¼ teaspoon freshly grated nutmeg
⅓ teaspoon ground cloves
½ teaspoon pure vanilla extract
½ teaspoon pure coconut extract
⅛ teaspoon fine sea salt

1.Preheat the air fryer to 180°C. In a large bowl, combine coconut oil, flour, eggs, sweetener, baking powder, and vanilla. Pour batter into an ungreased round nonstick baking dish. 2. Line the zone 1 with baking paper. 3. Mix the coconut flour, almond flour, baking powder, and baking soda in a large mixing bowl. 4. In another mixing bowl, stir together the eggs and coconut oil. Add the wet mixture to the dry mixture. 5. Mix in the remaining ingredients and stir until a soft dough forms. 6. Drop about 2 tablespoons of dough on the baking paper for each cookie and flatten each biscuit until it's 1 inch thick. 7. Place dish into the zone 2 . 8. Set the temperature to 200°C for the zone 1 and 150°C for the zone 2. Set the time to 25 minutes until the cookies are golden and firm to the touch. Select BAKE. Select START. 9. When done, shortcake should be golden, and a toothpick inserted in the middle will come out clean. 10. Remove dish from fryer and let cool 1 hour. 11. Once cooled, top cake with whipped cream and strawberries to serve. 12. Remove from the basket to a plate. Let the cookies cool to room temperature and serve.

Printed in Great Britain
by Amazon